DISCARD

WILLIAM TECUMSEH SHERMAN
Defender and Destroyer

WILLIAM TECUMSEH SHERMAN
Defender and Destroyer

Nancy Whitelaw

WILLIAM TECUMSEH SHERMAN *Defender and Destroyer*

Copyright © 1996 by Nancy Whitelaw

All rights reserved.
This book, or parts thereof, may not be reproduced in any form except by written consent of the publisher. For information write:
Morgan Reynolds, Inc., 803 S. Elam Ave., Greensboro, North Carolina 27403 USA

Library of Congress Cataloging-in-Publication Data
Whitelaw, Nancy.
  William Tecumseh Sherman : defender and destroyer / Nancy Whitelaw.
    p. cm. -- (Notable Americans)
  Includes bibliographical references and index.
  ISBN 1-883846-12-9
    1. Sherman, William T. (William Tecumseh), 1820-1891—Juvenile literature. 2. Generals--United States--Biography--Juvenile literature.   3. United States. Army--Biography--Juvenile literature.   I. Title II. Series
355'. 0092—dc20
[B]

95-26283
CIP

Printed in the United States of America
First Edition

Dedicated with love to Desi Vail

CONTENTS

Chapter One:
From Schoolboy to Second Lieutenant 9
Chapter Two
Enforcing Laws 16
Chapter Three
Banker, Major General, Lawyer,
School Superintendent 23
Chapter Four
Back In The Army 33
Chapter Five
Insane? 40
Chapter Six
Winning and Losing 48
Chapter Seven
Headed For Atlanta 58
Chapter Eight
Defender and Destroyer 66
Chapter Nine
The Smokey March 80
Chapter Ten
"Faithful and Honorable" 91
Timeline 101
Notes 102
Bibliography 107
Index 108

SHERMAN'S 1864-1865 CAMPAIGN

Chapter One
FROM SCHOOLBOY TO SECOND LIEUTENANT

Southern Whites called him a devil, the Union general whose armies looted and burned their way through the South, sparing neither adults nor children.

Reporters said he was insane.

William Tecumseh Sherman heard only his own conscience. That voice told him that he alone knew how to end the Civil War. Anyone who disagreed was at best misinformed, at worst a traitor.

He had a confident answer to anyone who questioned him: "If the people howl against my barbarity and cruelty, I will answer that war is war and not popularity-seeking."

Tecumseh Sherman was born in 1820 in Lancaster, Ohio. He was named after Indian Chief Tecumseh, a peace-maker. The red-haired, red-faced baby was immediately re-named Cump by his two brothers and three sisters. They could not bother with such a long name for their tiny brother.

Cump's father, Charles Sherman, was a lawyer, a judge, and a tax collector. The family lived in a comfortable two-story frame house in a town big enough to need a jail, a courthouse, a gunsmith, and a maker of spinning wheels. A stagecoach line passed through the town regularly, bringing occasional mail.

Cump had plenty of friends. The Shermans had eleven children in all. Their neighbors, the Ewings, had six youngsters. The Sherman and Ewing children were close friends, comfortable in each other's houses. They found plenty to do together—skating on Neibling's Pond, hunting rabbits in the woods, raising watermelons, caring for chickens, and making up running and chasing games.

They hunted for a "hoop" snake, an imaginary animal with an intense hatred for boys and a sharp poisonous horn in the middle of its head. When this snake saw a boy, it would catch its tail in its mouth. Then like a hoop, it would roll toward the boy and attack him ferociously.

It was Cump who figured out a way to save the chased boy and to punish the snake. If chased, a boy was to run straight for a tree. At the last moment, he was to turn away. The snake, unable to stop rolling, would bury its horn in the tree and perish. The snake would contribute to its own death, a proper punishment, said Cump.

He went to school in a brand new brick building which had recently replaced a log schoolhouse. Classes were difficult and included Latin, Greek, French, as well as reading, writing, and arithmetic. Cump was proud of being first in all his classes.

His biggest problem was his red hair. The other kids loved to tease him and call him Red-Headed Woodpecker. Cump decided to solve the problem by using his brain instead of his fists. He dyed his hair. But something went wrong—very wrong. His hair came out green. By the time it grew out, Cump decided that his hair wasn't that important after all. He didn't care much about how his clothes looked either. He had more important thinking to do.

Some of this thinking was about the hottest topic of the day—slavery. Cump listened to dinner table talk when his parents had guests. Questions spun around the table. Was slavery unconstitutional? Was slavery cruel? If a slave escaped, did he become a free man? Did a slave have rights?

Cump listened, and he learned. Half of the twenty-two states in the United States allowed slavery. Most of these were Southern states where slaves were particularly useful on large plantations. Most Southerners saw nothing wrong with slavery. The other eleven states, including Ohio, were "free states" where most citizens saw little need for slaves. Some of these citizens believed that slavery was cruel. Cump could see no reason for conflict. He thought that people who wanted slaves should have them. The others should mind their own business.

Cump was nine years old when his father died of a typhoid-like disease. At first the Sherman sons—Cump, 15-year-old Taylor, 14-year-old James, and 6-year-old John thought they could take care of their mother Mary, and the seven other children. They quickly learned that they could not possibly feed and clothe twelve people. Mary agreed that some of the children would have to live with other families.

Thomas Ewing and his wife Maria offered to take one child.

"You must give me the brightest of the lot," Mr. Ewing told Mary Sherman, "and I will make a man of him."

They chose Cump. He moved to the nearby brick mansion, and his stepfather and stepmother did everything they could to make him feel at home. Cump did not discuss the problem that bothered him all the time—his pride. He resented the fact that he was dependent on neighbors, no matter how gracious they were.

Before she accepted him, Mrs. Ewing wanted Cump baptized in the Roman Catholic Church. Cump and his mother agreed, but the priest objected. He could not bless the Indian name of Tecumseh. He suggested the name of William. The 10-year-old became William Tecumseh Sherman on official papers. He remained Cump to friends and family.

Thomas Ewing became a United States senator. On his trips home from Washington, he told his family about arguments in Congress. South Carolina representatives complained that the federal government favored Northerners. They threatened to secede, to break away from the United States. They said that other Southern states would join them in seceding. They would create a new country.

Ewing spoke against secession. He said that states must be loyal and obedient to the national government, commonly called the Union.

When he was fourteen, Cump got his first job. He worked as a rodman, a surveyor's assistant, for fifty cents a day. He enjoyed the work. He was tall and strong, and he liked being outdoors.

There was lots of work for a surveyor. Demand for roads was heavy. Long lines of Conestoga horse-drawn wagons rolled through Lancaster, pushing back the western frontier. The wagons brought pioneer families looking for adventure and land, and traders selling clothing, farm equipment, and other supplies.

Cump might have been happy as a surveyor for the rest of his life. But Ewing suggested that he enroll in West Point, a new military academy on the banks of the Hudson River in New York. Cump was

Defender and Destroyer

not particularly interested. He had never thought of becoming a soldier. He didn't care about guns except the rifles he used for hunting rabbits and squirrels. But his pride told him that he had a responsibility to obey Ewing. Without a complaint, he signed up for an eight-year term. He promised to spend four years as a student and four years in military service

Sixteen-year-old Cump left for West Point in May, 1836 in a horse-drawn coach. After three days of travel, he arrived in Fredericksburg, Maryland. Then he took a two-horse hack for the trip to Washington. There he stayed to see the sights that Ewing had talked about. He was thrilled to stand at the wood railing in front of the White House for an hour. From there he watched President Andrew Jackson pace up and down the gravel path in front of the mansion. After a few days seeing the sights, it was time to complete his travels to West Point.

The West Point campus was a group of run-down administration buildings, classrooms, and some barracks. Cump's uniform was a stiff gray coat with a stand-up collar, tight white trousers, and a black felt cap with a black pompon. His tiny room held only a cot and a chair. He was issued five items: an arithmetic book, a lamp, a bucket, a broom, and a pair of blankets.

As he watched evening parade for the first time, Cump was thrilled: "I felt the beauty of the Military parade and show—the fine music—the old cadets marching by in companies, stepping as one man, all forming in line, heard the roar of the evening gun and saw the flag fall and the parade dismissed, then my highest ambition was to be an old cadet."

The new cadets learned immediately that they would receive no respect on campus. Their role was to obey without question. After a roll-call at dawn, cadets rushed to give their rooms a thorough cleaning. After breakfast, they recited and studied until 1:00. Then they marched to dinner. By 2:00, they were back to their books. At 4:00 they left their classrooms to march, drill, handle muskets, and learn to follow the orders shouted at them. After supper, they studied until the bugler blew taps at sunset.

Many of the courses were typical high school subjects, including algebra, geometry, French, and literature. Students also studied basic information about artillery, infantry, and cavalry. Above all, they learned obedience and respect for authority.

Cump suffered most with regulations about cleanliness, neatness, and order. He earned demerits for improperly blackened shoes, a rusty belt buckle, dull coat buttons. He also received three demerits each time he was absent from roll call, and eight for each absence from a drill. He added to his total by speaking freely in class.

A few times when he was asked to recite, he said, "I can't do that, sir."

"Why not?"

"Well, to be frank, I haven't studied it."

More demerits!

His first year, Cump received 150 demerits. Any cadet who received more than 200 a year was expelled. "I was not considered a good soldier," he admitted.

Once, Cump asked his mother to lend him five dollars. "I would be the last person that would ask for it unless it were absolutely necessary, but you yourself know that it would be no means comfortable to walk post in the open air with a cold gun and thin gloves." He added, "I do not wish ever to ask Mr. Ewing again for assistance."

Cump and the other cadets learned to work with the system and even to get around it. They became clever about arranging after-hours parties. At supper in the dining room, they wrapped boiled potatoes in handkerchiefs, and hid them in their vests. They poked lumps of butter into their gloves. They stuffed their pockets with bread. After taps, Cump created a hash with the stolen food. They sat around, eating and telling stories. Most cadets agreed that Cump had the best imagination and was a pretty good cook, too.

Sometimes they put on casual clothes and sneaked away to a nearby restaurant. For a couple of hours, they enjoyed oysters and other special foods as they pretended they were civilians. Sometimes in their free time, they talked about current events. Slavery was still a hot topic. The cadets, trained to obey, generally agreed that problems about slavery arose because people disobeyed laws. These law-breakers were slaves who tried to escape and Abolitionists (anti-slavery people) who helped them to escape. Most cadets thought that Abolitionists should be fined or imprisoned. Punishment for runaway slaves would be decided by their masters.

Cump graduated from West Point in 1840, sixth in his class. A pretty good record, especially since more than half of those who entered the school in his class had dropped out or been expelled! Cump was proud of himself and eager to face the future. He was no longer a schoolboy, ready to lead his friends into pranks. He was Second Lieutenant Sherman, representing law and order in the service of his country.

Granted a three month's furlough, he spent the time in Lancaster with his family. He especially enjoyed the company of sixteen-year-old Ellen Ewing.

Chapter Two
ENFORCING LAWS

Sherman was assigned to the Third Artillery stationed on the swamps of Florida's east coast. Since there was no war in the country at that time, soldiers performed police duties.

In Florida, law-breakers included wandering Seminole Indians. Searching for more land and new opportunities, they traveled off the reservations where the government required them to live. Sometimes they built new villages before the government caught up with them. Sherman gave the Indians a choice. They could return to their reservation unharmed or he would destroy their property. When the troops found a village in an unapproved location, they burned the cabins and destroyed food supplies. Their morale broken, the Seminoles returned sadly but quietly to the land set aside for them. Without firing a shot, Sherman and his men accomplished their mission.

Sherman's assignment also included catching runaway slaves. His job was to return them to their masters in as good condition as possible. To accomplish this, he often used trickery instead of direct attacks.

Sherman spent happy and successful days on his horse, hunting down individuals and groups. He also enjoyed a lot of free time. He delighted in the clear warm water of the Indian River. The twenty-year-old soldier liked swimming, fishing, spearing sharks, and setting nets for green turtles. He collected pets. In his bedroom, a hen laid her eggs in one corner. A fawn slept on a bed of rushes in another corner. Crows roosted in a pile of brush he brought in for them.

As time passed, however, he grew discontented about his career. He had been out of West Point for over a year and had not yet fired a single shot in the service of his country. What's more, he didn't see any likelihood of military action in the future.

In June 1842, he was transferred to Fort Moultrie, near Charleston, South Carolina. His official duties were light. He worked on problems relating to military supplies.

He was bored with his work, but not with his life. Charleston was a model of southern culture, history, and snobbery. Impressive in his gold-buttoned blue uniform and erect military posture, Sherman attended parties, balls, horse races, and the theater and opera. He visited in many stately pillared homes of the well-to-do. Although he did not particularly care for this formal entertainment, he believed that it was his duty to keep open communications between the army and the Charleston residents.

Like his hosts, he enjoyed the easy life brought by slave labor, and he saw no reason to do away with slavery. He sometimes wished that some masters treated their slaves more kindly. But this was just a passing thought, unimportant since the masters were breaking no laws.

In Sherman's mind, the law-breakers were the Abolitionists. These men and women, mostly Northerners, were no better than common thieves. They conspired to take property—slaves—from owners who had bought and paid for them.

Sherman couldn't understand why some people said that slavery was unconstitutional. He said the Constitution allowed a citizen to own property. Slaves were property, so owning them could not be unconstitutional.

Although Sherman agreed with Southerners on slavery, he was horrified by their talk of secession. William Tecumseh Sherman believed that such talk was treason.

Sherman stayed in the South for five years. He loved Southern culture and tradition. But he was impatient with the lack of excitement and purpose in his military career. Also, he wanted to get married. Ellen Ewing had become a beautiful young lady with soft black hair, blue eyes, and self-confidence. They were in love. He thought about quitting the military. He could not support a wife comfortably on his military pay of seventy dollars a month, especially since he sent some of that to his mother. His brother John was a lawyer, and Sherman might have followed in his footsteps, but he didn't like the idea of speaking in public. He had no choice but to stay in the military until he had another definite career in mind.

He was next assigned to Pittsburgh, Pennsylvania. This sounded good at first. He would be closer to Lancaster and Ellen. He would be involved in recruiting for active duty in Mexico where Americans and Texans were fighting over boundaries. At last—an opportunity to serve his country in a military role.

Within a few months, he was bored again. His military role was indirect. He didn't want to recruit soldiers to fight. He wanted to take part in the fighting himself. He wrote to the Adjutant-General, asking to be sent on an expedition, a hazardous one, if possible.

Defender and Destroyer

He was sure that he deserved to be chosen. So he didn't wait for an answer. He went to Cincinnati with some recruits. There he told the officer in charge to give him orders to take the recruits on to Texas.

The officer refused. Further, he reprimanded Sherman and sent him back to Pittsburgh. Sherman had no choice but to obey.

A short time after he arrived back in Pittsburgh, he received orders to proceed to California. As in Texas, Americans and Mexicans were fighting over land in California. Delighted with the possibility of battle, Sherman travelled to New York. There he boarded the U.S.S *Lexington* for the 200-day trip around Cape Horn to California. Time passed slowly on the ship. Sherman was eager to get into the fighting.

Finally the ship docked in Monterey Bay, California. All hands welcomed the sight of green grass and whitewashed adobe houses. Before landing, they readied their swords and gave their guns a last-minute oiling. But they were too late. The Mexicans had fled to the hills.

Instead of a fighter, Sherman became a quarter-master. He was responsible for housing, food, and supplies. He kept the commissary supplied with wild fowl, deer, and elk. He erected sawmills, gristmills, and other industries to make the post self-supporting. He was busy, but once again bored. His love of riding and exploring saved him from complete frustration. Whenever he could, Sherman rode around the countryside, sometimes hunting deer and bear in the mountains, sometimes ducks and geese on the plains.

He wrote to Ellen: "I have felt tempted to send my resignation to Washington ... after having passed through a war without smelling gunpowder ...." His despair increased when he heard news of former West Point classmates promoted for their bravery and skill in battles.

These men had become captains, majors, and colonels. Sherman remained a first lieutenant.

"Gold fever" spread through California after the discovery of gold in the Sacramento River in 1848. One man collected $40,000 in seven weeks. Two partners collected $17,000 in one week. A young boy found $2,700 in just two days. Fortune seekers came west from all over the country. Some came overland in covered wagons. Some sailed all the way around South America. Others sailed to Central America, walked through jungles to the west coast and then sailed on to California.

Sherman did not catch the "fever." He had joined the army with a vow to be loyal. He would not break that vow for all the gold in California. However, many military men became so infected that they deserted their posts. They could earn $25 a day, digging for prospectors, $18 more than their military pay.

The desertions changed Sherman's assignment. He was charged with bringing back deserters. This was familiar work for Sherman. He had chased down wandering Seminoles and runaway slaves. He was confident, and he was proud of his responsibility to bring lawbreakers to justice.

After some months in this work, Sherman took a sixty-day furlough to work as a surveyor. Using skills he had first learned when he was fourteen, Sherman earned six thousand dollars.

Still, he was not fulfilled. His West Point dreams of fighting for his country remained just dreams. If only he could think of another career, he would quit the army in a minute. Three years after arriving in California, he was assigned to New York to carry special messages for General Winfield Scott. Maybe this was his chance to become involved with secret messages and military strategies. At the least,

Defender and Destroyer

Ellen Ewing Sherman

it would take him closer to Ellen.

He left California on January 2, 1850. On May 1, he and twenty-six-year old Ellen were married, finally ending their eight-year engagement.

After a six-month furlough, Sherman returned to work, promoted to captain. The promotion pleased him, but his work did not. Once again, Sherman found himself with lots of free time and no job satisfaction. He spent hours in the Senate gallery, listening to Ewing and other Senators debating about slavery.

Sherman's views remained the same. Men had a right to own slaves but they should not abuse them. The Union was more important than any state or group of states.

In the fall of 1850, Sherman was assigned to St. Louis, Missouri. Ellen arrived in February, 1851 with their first child, a daughter named Maria "Minnie" Ewing Sherman. Their rented house delighted Ellen with its modern conveniences—gas fixtures and indoor plumbing. It was the outdoors that beckoned to her husband. He enjoyed cattle-buying trips on the Missouri and Kansas plains. He liked the strenuous riding, sleeping under the stars, and living in the open. But his job as quarter-master bored him. And he was always short of money. "My household expenses are beyond my means," he confided to his brother. He was ashamed. Would money always be a problem? He was embarrassed that he could not treat the Ewing's daughter as well as the Ewings had treated him.

His problem was not just financial. Ellen remained dependent on her parents for attention and moral support. When she became pregnant again, she went back to Lancaster. Sherman's pride was hurt. He wanted Ellen to depend on him, not on the Ewings.

Chapter Three
BANKER, MAJOR GENERAL, LAWYER, SCHOOL SUPERINTENDENT

Lonesome, Sherman brooded about his life. He had failed to find glory and excitement in the military. He had failed to support his wife as she wanted. He had no prospects of a better future.

He was assigned to New Orleans, Louisiana. His task was to stop corruption in the commissary. The job scarcely interested him, but he looked forward to living in the South again.

Sherman soon had two infant daughters. Ellen came to New Orleans with Minnie and new-born Mary Elizabeth (Lizzie) for Christmas. Sherman hoped that Ellen would not hurry back to her parents in Lancaster.

Even with his family beside him, Sherman was restless. He found little satisfaction in his daily work. His financial problems increased because living in New Orleans was much more expensive than living in St. Louis. Ellen begged him to leave the army for a more promising career.

He saw a gleam of hope when friends offered him a partnership in a bank in San Francisco, California. His salary would be more than twice as much as he earned in the army. He accepted cautiously, taking only a six-month leave from the army. By March 1853,

Sherman was on a ship headed for San Francisco, by way of Nicaragua in Central America. Ellen returned to Lancaster, not ready to travel across the country with two babies.

In San Francisco, prospects looked even better than Sherman had expected. The city was alive with land speculators and other investors, building projects, and trading.

In September 1853, he decided that banking was the career for him. The money made the work worthwhile even though he disliked the idea of a desk job. Thirty-three-year-old Sherman resigned from the army after 17 years of service. With some regret, he packed away his sword and sash.

He returned to Lancaster for his family. The Ewings didn't want Ellen and the daughters to leave. Under this family pressure, Ellen doubted if she should make the trip. Sherman's pride hung in the balance as they argued back and forth. Finally and reluctantly, the Ewings made a decision. Ellen and the younger baby could go. Minnie would stay in Lancaster. Unwillingly, Sherman agreed. He could not yet stand on his own two feet in front of the Ewings.

Right from the first day, Ellen disliked San Francisco. She missed her family. She hated the dirty streets, decrepit buildings, noisy merchants and adventurers, and the ever-present flies.

They faced health problems. Sherman had been bothered by asthma off and on during his life. Now he lay awake night after night, gasping for breath. Ellen suffered from persistent headaches affecting her both physically and emotionally. The baby caught colds in the damp and chilly house.

Again, the Shermans did not have enough money to meet expenses. San Francisco living was far more expensive than they had

Defender and Destroyer

Sherman with his son Thomas Ewing

expected. Sherman disapproved of the way Ellen spent money for clothes, furniture, and entertainment.

In June 1854, William (Willie) Ewing Sherman arrived. More than ever, Ellen missed the comfort and security of living with her parents. She yearned for their help in caring for Lizzie and newborn Willie. She would have left within weeks except that Sherman convinced her to stay until Willie was old enough to travel more easily.

Back in Ohio, Sherman's brother John became a member of Congress. John ran on an anti-slavery platform. Sherman wrote to him, warning him not to accept the popular Northern attitude toward slavery. He urged John to allow Southerners to retain the slaves they needed to create a sound economy.

That year, bad debts forced many California banks to close. Because Sherman had managed his firm with caution, his bank remained stable. Sherman was proud of what he had done for the bank. He was able to assure panicky investors and depositors that their savings were safe. But Sherman once again suffered from severe asthma attacks, probably due to stress.

Sherman became one of San Francisco's best known bankers. He had confidence in himself as a businessman. So did others. California Governor J. Neely Johnson asked for his help. Corruption of public officials created severe problems in law and order. Looting and pillaging became so common that citizens formed a vigilante group to protect themselves and their property. Governor Johnson asked Sherman to fight against the vigilante groups. Sherman eagerly accepted appointment as major general in the state militia.

Sherman announced that the vigilantes had a choice. They could

Mary Elizabeth Sherman

Rachael and Eleanor Sherman

stop their illegal activities, or they could face punishment from him and his troops. They chose to continue their activities.

Sherman called out the National Guard. He asked General Wool, the head of the federal arsenal, to fill his request for muskets, cartridge boxes, and other supplies. Wool refused. Sherman could not force him. Shocked and angry, he resigned, vowing never again to work in public affairs.

In the fall of 1856 a new son, Thomas Ewing Sherman, arrived. The baby's namesake wrote from Ohio, offering to pay Sherman's expenses if he would come back East to live. Sherman declined. He would not back out of his responsibility to the bank. Besides, he did not want to be dependent on his father-in-law again.

The next spring, the California offices of the bank were closed, despite Sherman's pleas. He accepted an offer to represent the firm in New York City.

In May, 1857, Sherman left his family at Lancaster. He traveled on to New York. He could only hope that this job would be better than the last one.

Again, a banking crisis occurred, and again Sherman's bank faced trouble. Sherman lamented, "wherever I go there is a breakdown." In January, he had to close the bank. He was left with no banking career, no military career, no prospects at all. He had a growing family to support. His wife was happier with her parents than with him.

Swallowing his pride, Sherman asked his father-in-law for help. Ewing happily agreed to give temporary financial help and a job. Humiliated, Sherman accepted both.

In the summer of 1858, Sherman rejoined his family in Ohio.

They left in the fall for Leavenworth, Kansas where Ewing carried

Sherman as Superintendant of the Louisiana Military Seminary

on a law practice and also bought and sold real estate.

Sherman thought again about becoming a lawyer. In that career, he might be able to break away from Ewing and work on his own. With no training, he was admitted to the bar "on the ground of general intelligence and reputation."

Sherman served in court only once. During the trial, the opposing lawyer called Sherman a robber. Sherman flew into a rage and threatened to beat him up. He lost the case and decided never to practice law again.

Next, he worked as manager for Ewing's properties. He cleared land, built cabins, and supervised workmen. He enjoyed the outdoor work, riding over the sparsely populated country to survey and record plot boundaries.

Ellen returned to Lancaster to await the birth of their fifth child. Would she be dependent on the Ewings all her life?

Lonely, Sherman wandered around the military grounds in Leavenworth. Stirring memories of West Point flooded his mind. Maybe his heart belonged in the military after all.

He contacted a friend from West Point asking for a job as army paymaster. The friend, Major D. C. Buell, said no. Instead, he offered him a job as superintendent of a military academy in Louisiana. This could be the perfect career for Sherman. He accepted eagerly, glad to be involved with the military and eager to live in the South again.

The only problem was that he believed the South was not a good place for Ellen and the children. He believed that soon the streets would not be safe. Abolitionists encouraged slaves to run away. Although masters tightened plantation security, the slaves could not be contained. The underground railroad offered freedom to those who dared make a run for it. Slave owners carried arms at all times. Who knew when slaves might seize these guns and knives?

The situation had grown more tense after 1857 when Dred Scott, a slave, was taken by his master to Minnesota, a free state. Scott declared that he was a free man because he had lived in a free state. The Supreme Court ruled that Scott could never be free. They also ruled that Scott, because of his race, did not have the right to sue for his freedom. The Constitution did not apply to him, according to the Supreme Court. The ruling was a victory for pro-slavery forces. Abolitionists fought even harder to have slavery outlawed throughout the country.

In 1859, Abolitionist John Brown had attacked the federal weapons arsenal at Harpers Ferry, Virginia. Although Brown was captured and hung, his raid created fear of more uprisings, particularly among Southerners.

Further agitation came from Abraham Lincoln, an increasingly popular Republican leader. Lincoln declared that the country could not exist half-slave and half-free. In that case, the southerners believed, the country could not exist at all. Many Southerners were ready to form their own country, an act they called disunion.

For himself, Sherman hoped to ignore the conflict. He had strong views as he wrote his father-in-law: "I would not if I could abolish or modify slavery ... still, of course I wish it never had existed, for it does make mischief." More important to Sherman was the Union: "The true position for every gentleman North and South is to frown down even a mention of Disunion."

Sherman had not time to spend on politics. He was determined not to fail at this new career. Although hired as superintendent, his first task was to build the school. He supervised carpenters who made tables, benches, desks, and chairs. He conferred with state officials about regulations. He hired instructors and acquired funding for laboratories. He set up drill and regimentation schedules. He persuaded the Secretary of War in Washington to provide muskets and ammunition for the school arsenal.

The Louisiana Military Seminary opened on New Year's Day, 1860. Forty-year-old William Sherman became both principal and teacher of the first nineteen cadets.

Sherman was tall and angular with bright hazel eyes and auburn hair. Students said that a tuft of hair stood out straight when he became excited. Far away from his own sons, Sherman became a father to many of the cadets. He listened to their problems and cared for them when they were sick.

Those students who broke regulations saw another side of this "father." Some complained to their parents that Sherman was too strict. Sherman told cadets and parents alike they could either accept the discipline or leave the school.

His colleagues asked him jokingly if he was related to the Congressman John Sherman who spoke out strongly for abolition. "Only a brother," Sherman joked back. He defended John's right to his beliefs.

Both Sherman and Ellen decided that they must have the family together again. Sherman made plans to build a house. He wrote to Ellen about living arrangements, telling her they would use slaves, not servants, like all other Southerners.

Chapter Four
BACK IN THE ARMY

In November 1860, Abraham Lincoln won the presidential election. Sherman saw both good and bad in this. He agreed with Lincoln's position that the federal government should not interfere with slavery. He supported Lincoln's pledge to keep the states united. But he could not agree with Lincoln's view that the sectional conflict would be settled without bloodshed. Sherman had seen war preparations in the South, and he had talked with Southerners. He predicted a long and agonizing war.

As soon as Sherman heard the election returns, he wrote Ellen that she should stay in Ohio. He feared open political battles in the South. He predicted that vigilantes might take over in the South as they had in California.

In late 1860 and early 1861, Alabama and Mississippi followed South Carolina's lead and voted to secede. Sherman believed that Louisiana would be next. He wrote to Governor Thomas Moore:

"If Louisiana withdraws from the Federal Union,
I prefer to maintain my allegiance to the
constitution as long as a fragment of it survives
....on no earthly account will I do any act or

think any thought hostile or in defiance to the old government of the United States."

Moore asked Sherman to reconsider. He could not—would not—change his mind.

In January 1861, Louisiana troops took over the U. S. Arsenal at Baton Rouge. They asked Sherman to store the arsenal's weapons at the seminary. Sherman refused to accept what he called stolen property.

In February, Sherman's worst fears became reality. Jefferson Davis became president of the new Confederate States of America (CSA). Louisiana broke from the USA to join the CSA, which now included South Carolina, Mississippi, Florida, Alabama, Georgia, and Texas.

On February 19, Sherman left the college. He shook hands with each cadet. When he reached the line of professors he merely pointed to his heart and whispered, "You are all here." To the governor, he said, "I hope that if I should go into the army, I'll not catch you, for I should surely hang you." Saying that "The United States seems to be melting away like a snowball in the sun," Sherman left the South. He was eager to be with his family again, but despairing over the future of his country.

In March, Sherman was in Lancaster without a job and unable to support his family. Although he hated to ask for help, he turned to his brother John, now a senator. John encouraged Sherman to get back in the military, and he took him to visit President Lincoln. Sherman told Lincoln that he feared serious problems from the South.

"Oh, well, I guess we'll manage to keep house," answered Lincoln calmly.

Defender and Destroyer

Senator John Sherman

Shocked, Sherman offered his services in the conflict he knew would come.

"We shall not need many men like you, the affair will soon blow over," answered Lincoln.

Outside the White House, Sherman lost his temper. "The North just don't care a damn, you politicians have got things in a hell of a fix!" he told his brother.

Sherman was disgusted with Northerners for their indifference. He was disgusted with Southerners for their hostility. The West remained the only place for him to go.

He accepted a job as president of street car railway in St. Louis, Missouri. Almost immediately, he reduced operating costs by 20 percent. As a manager, he was efficient and effective. But he was bored, and, as always, he was not making enough money to support his family in the way he wanted to.

In April 1861, the Confederates fired the opening shots of the Civil War at Fort Sumter in the harbor of Charleston, South Carolina. Lincoln called for 75,000 volunteers. This would be a short war, he said. Sherman scoffed. He said that Lincoln should have called for at least 300,000 men. He should have called for regular soldiers, not volunteers. It would be "a long war—very long—much longer than any politician thinks," he predicted.

Despite his reservations about Lincoln's judgement, Sherman answered in May when Lincoln called for soldiers. He was appointed colonel in the Thirteenth Regular Infantry.

He retrieved his sword, saddle, and sash from the trunk where he laid it eight years ago. Once again, Sherman was eager to serve his country!

Pregnant again, Ellen took the children back "home" to Lancaster

Defender and Destroyer

when Sherman received orders to proceed to Washington, D.C.

Sherman's eagerness to serve vanished when he received his assignment to train volunteers. The assignment made sense to military officials—a graduate of West Point and a former headmaster of a military school would be perfect for training recruits. But Sherman wanted to fight, not to train others to fight.

Most of the recruits were young men with no military experience. Worse, they saw no reason for strict military discipline and drill. Few expected to fight. They looked for adventure and fun in the capital of their country. They had signed up for the required three months, and they meant to leave with happy memories of new experiences and new friends.

They were not impressed with their new commander at first sight. One described Sherman: "a tall gaunt form clad in a thread bare blue coat, the sleeves so short as to reveal a long stretch of bony wrist, the trousers at least four inches less than the usual length ..." They said he looked more like a farmer than an army officer, especially when he wore a broad-brimmed straw hat. They quickly learned the difference between Sherman's looks and his attitude. He forced the soldiers to drill for hours on end. He shouted until his voice was hoarse. The more he shouted, the more they resisted, and the angrier he became. Sherman was driven by the thought of these young men in battle. He believed that training and discipline would be their strongest weapons. He was determined to furnish them with these weapons.

In late June, Sherman was ordered to march his regiments to Virginia to prevent the Southern armies from overtaking Washington, D. C. His troops weren't ready for battle, and Sherman knew it.

They lacked sufficient discipline, training, uniforms, and arms. But he had to follow orders.

He marched the troops down the hot dusty roads near Bull Run Creek in northern Virginia. They complained about heat, dust, and weariness. They paid little attention to their superiors who urged them to stand straight and tall, to march along at a steady pace, and to think of their responsibility to their country.

Sherman learned that some soldiers in the rear broke from the ranks to search for water, berries, and other food. Others stole food from houses along the way. Enraged, Sherman sent messengers to tell the men to stay in formation. The soldiers sent back a message. "Tell Colonel Sherman we'll be havin' all the water, pigs, and chickens we want!"

The troops straggled on. Near Bull Run, they faced Confederate troops led by General Pierre Beauregard. These troops were as untrained, undisciplined, and inexperienced as Sherman's troops.

They met in battle, both sides struggling with unskilled men and horses, broken-down wagons, misfiring cannons, and panic and chaos. Soon, streams of wounded men were limping and crawling back to their regiments.

Trying to push his men forward into battle, Sherman was under heavy fire for hours. At one point, his horse was shot out from under him.

Through the smoke of cannons, rifles, and muskets, Sherman spotted some of his troops retreating. Wounded and fearful, Union soldiers hoped to retreat back to Washington. Sherman gave them a choice. They could re-join the regiment and fight as they should. Or they could stay where they were and be killed by Confederate fire.

Defender and Destroyer

Most chose to re-join the Union troops.

When he found deserters, Sherman made the punishment stricter. Anyone found escaping faced several days of very intense drill. A lieutenant described Sherman's attitude: "They [the soldiers] became clamorous for food. Sherman sneered at them for such unsoldierly conduct. They begged for some place to rest. He bade them sleep on the ground. They had no blankets, many not even a jacket, and all were shivering and wet... Sherman called them 'a pack of New York loafers and thieves.'"

Sherman refused to talk to reporters, claiming that their reports would help the enemy. Sherman would not let anything interfere with his chances for success.

But his first battle did not bring success. The Battle of Bull Run ended with hundreds on both sides wounded or killed. Sherman was disgusted with himself. He had failed to lead his troops to victory. He did not appreciate his promotion to brigadier-general of volunteers. He accepted it, but requested that Lincoln never again leave him in a position of authority. Lincoln laughed. He said it was the first time any officer had made such a request.

After the battle, many of Sherman's soldiers prepared to go home. They had enlisted for only three months, they said, and their time was up. Sherman told them they could go back to the camp or be shot leaving it. Many soldiers protested. Sherman imprisoned a hundred protestors. He said he would shoot anybody else who complained. He heard no more complaints.

Chapter Five
INSANE?

Sherman was next assigned to Kentucky. His job was to organize Kentuckians into fighting units. The units would protect all-important transportation routes along the Mississippi River and in the growing railroad network.

From his base in Louisville, Sherman sent out the word that he needed 100,000 men immediately. He did this although he knew such a large number of recruits were not available.

After some small battles around Louisville, Sherman complained to his superiors that he had been given 4000 men to fight against an enemy force of 15,000. He declared that his camp was infested with spies. He refused again to allow reporters in the camp. He complained that it was impossible to train the lazy irresponsible recruits that were sent to him, that he had to contend with undisciplined recruits, poor food, contaminated water, and faulty weapons.

Like the soldiers at Bull Run, some Western recruits stole food from neighboring farms. First, Sherman warned against this stealing, called foraging. When his warning failed to end the practice he acted. A private stole a cow. Sherman sentenced the young man to death. Few soldiers foraged after that.

One day Sherman criticized a volunteer for not wearing a uniform. The young man protested, "A general with such a hat as you have on had no right to talk ..." Sherman seemed surprised to find that he was wearing a battered stove-pipe hat. He laughed and said, "Young man, you are right about the hat, but you ought to have your uniform."

Sherman's soldiers faced Confederate soldiers in small skirmishes on the outskirts of Louisville. Sherman expected a major battle at any moment. He sent a message to his adjutant general asking for at least 60,000 men. The answer came back: capture the Cumberland gap and proceed into East Tennessee. Sherman was astounded. He had asked for more men. The answer was the he should do even more with those he had.

Bypassing his superiors, he wrote to President Lincoln asking for additional men. He ended his letter with "Answer!" He received no answer.

He asked Secretary of War Simon Cameron to visit him right away "on business as important as any in Washington." Cameron came. Sherman showed him a map of the United States and pointed out how much territory he, Sherman, was responsible for. He argued that he needed 60,000 men at once and probably 200,000 before long.

Cameron threw up his hands. "Great God! Where are they to come from," he asked.

Sherman answered that plenty of men in the North were eager to fight. He sent letters to other Washington officials: "...our force here is out of all proportion to the position. Our defeat would be disastrous to the nation; and to expect of new men, who never bore arms, to do miracles, is not right."

A few weeks later, he saw a newspaper report of his meeting with

Cameron. The Secretary was quoted as saying that Sherman was "crazy, insane, and mad."

This language appealed to reporters who were looking for a sensational story. Some were particularly pleased to write against Sherman because he had often refused them interviews. They added to the furor by including reports from some of Sherman's men. The list of so-called strange behaviors was long. He smoked too much. Sometimes he didn't speak at all. Sometimes he spoke too much. He lied about troop numbers and supplies. He said that female nurses were a nuisance. He was too kind to Southerners. He dressed carelessly. He disciplined his troops harshly. As he talked, he drummed on a table, fidgeted with his buttons, "combed" his beard with his fingers. "His eye had a half-wild expression," wrote one reporter. Headlines of a Cincinnati paper blared: "General William T. Sherman Insane." Shocked, frustrated, and in despair, Sherman refused to speak to reporters at all. He imprisoned one who refused to leave.

General-in-Chief George McClellan ordered Sherman to send a daily report, specifically outlining his troop numbers and positions. Sherman refused. He said he did not have time to compose such a report. McClellan sent an aide to check up on Sherman. That aide reported that Sherman was too unsteady for any command and that Louisville was in no danger at all.

None of Sherman's colleagues could explain his problem. Possibly he suffered from exhaustion. Clearly, he was experiencing an emotional break-down.

Sherman asked to be relieved of his command. His request was granted. In his mind, he added one more failure to his record.

Defender and Destroyer

Disturbed by the reports, Ellen and the two boys visited Sherman. They found him sleepless, melancholy, and eating very little. They left after a few weeks, hoping that their visit had soothed his tired mind and soul.

In November 1861, Sherman had another chance to prove himself. He was sent to St. Louis to work under General Henry Halleck. They would fight against Confederates and also train new Union recruits. Although the military situation was not as serious as in Kentucky, Sherman kept up a noisy campaign for more troops, more supplies, more offensive moves. He fired off telegrams to Union generals, criticizing them for failure to attack, poor planning, and underestimating the enemy.

From letters and newspaper articles, Ellen realized that her visit had not been enough. Her husband was in serious trouble. She begged him to come home for a rest. A commanding officer agreed, writing that Sherman's "physical and mental system is so completely broken by labor and care as to render him for the present entirely unfit for duty...."

Overwhelmed with shame, Sherman agreed. He believed he had reached the depths of despair. His fellow officers and soldiers under him thought he was mad. Journalists called him a traitor. His wife had to bring him home as though he were a little boy in trouble at school. Worse still, he was once again dependent on his father-in-law for care and for money. Sherman arrived in Lancaster, his red beard streaked with gray, a dazed expression in his eyes, and skeleton thin. "I do think I should have committed suicide," he told John, "were it not for my children."

When his twenty-day leave was up, Sherman had to make a

decision. He could stay in the military and work with soldiers who criticized him and made fun of him. Or he could swallow his pride and ask his father-in-law for a job.

He chose the military. General Halleck assigned him to Paducah, Kentucky. Once again, Sherman's job was to prepare volunteers for active duty. He vowed to overcome his bad reputation by hard work. This time he worked under General Ulysses S. Grant. Sherman respected Grant, a fellow West Point graduate. Like Sherman, Grant had suffered from depression. Sherman hoped that Grant would be a role model for him.

Tirelessly, Sherman worked with the recruits. He studied the terrain and planned both defensive and offensive moves. He read all he could about both Confederate and Union strategies. He took charge of transportation of supplies and troops, using skills he had learned in California and St. Louis. He even talked to reporters. When they asked him what he thought of the military future in Kentucky, he answered, "We are in great danger." They asked why he didn't tell this to Grant and other superiors. "Oh, they'd call me crazy again," he replied.

By February 1862, Sherman was leading his troops in battle, first near Cairo, Illinois and then on to Fort Donelson, another important Confederate base. Finally, Sherman was beginning to regain confidence in himself.

In March, he received orders to destroy a railroad bridge and railroad connections near Corinth, Mississippi. As he and his troops neared their targets, heavy rain sent the river waters rising at the rate of six inches an hour. Flood-swollen streams prevented them from reaching the tracks. They had to unharness the horses from the artillery wagons to let them swim free. The soldiers dragged the heavy

Defender and Destroyer

General Ulysses S. Grant

guns under water back to the bank.

Defeated by the weather, they pitched camp at Shiloh Meetinghouse in southwestern Tennessee. Other Union divisions camped nearby, creating a force of 33,000 federal soldiers. Spring rains pounded on tents, and turned the grounds into mud. Soldiers were served mixtures of rice, flour, grease, salt, and water which could hardly be called food. Most men suffered from dysentery. No medicine was available.

At dawn on April 6, Confederate troops dashed out of the woods, guns blazing, bayonets aimed at Union soldiers. Sherman jumped onto his horse, shouting to his men to follow him, to fire, to keep up their courage. On every side, men and horses were falling. The air hummed with flying bullets. Men screamed in pain, shouted in anger, and cried. No doctors or ambulances were available. Sherman rode up and down the front of his lines, reforming regiments as fast as he could. At times soldiers were shooting at an enemy less than thirty feet away.

Four horses were shot out from under Sherman. A piece of buckshot lodged in his palm. Without taking his eyes off the enemy, he wrapped a handkerchief around the wound. He returned to his men, hat in tatters, red beard smeared with powder, and hand bandaged. His troops put their hats on their bayonets and waved them in a salute to him.

After three days of fighting, the Confederates withdrew. Sherman awoke the next day in a bullet-ridden tent. All around him soldiers were burying the dead, shoveling mangled and rotting corpses into hastily dug ditches. They covered them with dirt as quickly as they could.

Defender and Destroyer

General Ulysses S. Grant

guns under water back to the bank.

Defeated by the weather, they pitched camp at Shiloh Meetinghouse in southwestern Tennessee. Other Union divisions camped nearby, creating a force of 33,000 federal soldiers. Spring rains pounded on tents, and turned the grounds into mud. Soldiers were served mixtures of rice, flour, grease, salt, and water which could hardly be called food. Most men suffered from dysentery. No medicine was available.

At dawn on April 6, Confederate troops dashed out of the woods, guns blazing, bayonets aimed at Union soldiers. Sherman jumped onto his horse, shouting to his men to follow him, to fire, to keep up their courage. On every side, men and horses were falling. The air hummed with flying bullets. Men screamed in pain, shouted in anger, and cried. No doctors or ambulances were available. Sherman rode up and down the front of his lines, reforming regiments as fast as he could. At times soldiers were shooting at an enemy less than thirty feet away.

Four horses were shot out from under Sherman. A piece of buckshot lodged in his palm. Without taking his eyes off the enemy, he wrapped a handkerchief around the wound. He returned to his men, hat in tatters, red beard smeared with powder, and hand bandaged. His troops put their hats on their bayonets and waved them in a salute to him.

After three days of fighting, the Confederates withdrew. Sherman awoke the next day in a bullet-ridden tent. All around him soldiers were burying the dead, shoveling mangled and rotting corpses into hastily dug ditches. They covered them with dirt as quickly as they could.

Defender and Destroyer

General Halleck sent a wire to Secretary of War Cameron: "It is the unanimous opinion here that Brig. Gen. W. T. Sherman saved the fortune of the day on the 6th and contributed largely to the glorious victory on the 7th ...."

Sherman was promoted to major-general of the volunteers. He said of the battle: "...the scenes on this field would have cured anybody of war. Mangled bodies, dead, dying in every conceivable shape, without heads, legs; and horses!" He wrote to his father-in-law personally. He wanted to be sure that Ewing heard of his success.

Sherman asked Ellen to save all newspaper clippings that mentioned his name. One of these described Sherman: "Built narrow and almost effeminate, voluble and smiling, eyes light gray and flashing incessantly in every direction, ... he walked, talked or laughed all over ... I found Sherman pleasant and affable to his inferiors and engaging his equals with a mood that shifted like a barometer in a tropic sea."

Sherman was ordered to chase the retreating Confederates as they fled south into Mississippi. On April 27, he planned a surprise attack just outside Corinth. Two cannon shots signaled the attack. Sherman's troops rushed into the Confederate camp.

After several days of fighting, the Confederates retreated. Sherman was praised for strategy, bravery, and the discipline of his troops. He stayed in Corinth, repairing railroad bridges and trestles and setting up a supply depot.

Chapter Six
WINNING AND LOSING

In July 1862, Sherman was called to Memphis, Tennessee where the Confederate mayor had surrendered after much damage had been inflicted on the city. Sherman became military governor, assigned to the task of repairing war damage and insuring that the Confederates could not regain control there.

He ordered that stores and hotels re-open and that citizens return to their peacetime businesses. He offered all citizens an opportunity to take an oath of allegiance to the Union. He accepted runaway slaves as workers, keeping careful records so that masters could reclaim their slaves when the emergency passed.

Guerrillas sniped at patrols, burned bridges, and fired on ships. Sherman had neither time nor manpower to hold trials for every suspected guerilla. He told Mayor John Park that "the military for the time being must be superior to the civil authority." When guerrillas fired on a supply train, he ordered the arrest of "twenty-five of the most prominent men in the vicinity." When rebels fired on Union ships along the Arkansas River, he ordered his troops to destroy all houses, farms, and cornfields for 15 miles along the river bank. When snipers fired on a river steamship near Randolph, Sherman declared that ten families would be expelled from Mississippi for each boat fired on.

Southerners, and some Northerners, objected loudly. They said that rules of war allowed fighting against soldiers, not against civilians. Sherman declared that the Confederates had been the first to break the rules of war by encouraging civilians to be spies, guerrillas, and snipers.

Sherman's attitude toward the war had changed after the terrible battle at Shiloh. During the months after Fort Sumter, he thought the way to end the war quickly was to avoid as much destruction as possible. Perhaps when the leaders of the revolt realized the North did not want to destroy the South they would reconsider their decision to secede and decide to rejoin the union. But as the war continued, and the battles became more deadly, he realized most Confederate leaders would never change their minds. The only way to end the fighting was to make it to expensive, and painful, to continue. It gave him confidence that General Grant seemed to agree with his ideas on how to win the war.

Sherman was also now more confident in his ability to command troops, to discipline captured civilians, and even to talk to reporters. He let the journalists know that he no longer feared them. He gave them a choice. They could either write what he wanted them to write, or he would censor their reports. "You boys had better be careful what you write or I will be down on you."

In December, he was ordered to head toward Vicksburg, Mississippi to attack this well-fortified city on the Mississippi River. By December 19, Sherman had settled over 30,000 men on transports and gunboats near Chickasaw, about ten miles from Vicksburg. They faced heavy shelling from Confederates. Pilots struggled to navigate in heavy fog that concealed ships, landmarks, and jutting rocks. Wending their way through twisting bayous, many navigators lost their sense of direction. They became separated from the other troops.

After three miserable days, Sherman gave up. He retreated with a tragic record of 1700 men dead, wounded, or missing.

Sherman suffered for all the families who lost loved ones in the war. He wrote to Ellen: "Indeed I wish I had been killed long since."

He received orders to attack Arkansas Post, a fort on the Arkansas River. He planned a surprise attack on January 10 1863. The night before, he crawled as close as he dared to enemy lines. He listened and watched for signs that the Confederates had been warned. He found none. The next morning, the attack went off as planned.

For two days of fighting Sherman was in the front lines. Then the Confederates flew the white flag of surrender. Sherman entered the fort. He ordered the colonel in charge to have his men stack their arms, form a brigade, and wait for his orders. The colonel obeyed. Sherman pointed out to the defeated Confederate troops that the colonel had made the right choice. If he had chosen to continue to fight, he and his troops would have faced a humiliating defeat.

Sherman learned that newspaper reporters questioned his decision to launch the attack at Chickasaw. They asked: Had Sherman lost his sanity again?

In disgust, Sherman court-martialed a reporter who may have disguised himself as a soldier. He said the man would be tried in a military court since he was discovered in Union troop lines. Sherman threatened to resign if the man were not severely punished. At a trial in February, the reporter was banned from the group of journalists

Defender and Destroyer

Sherman with the officers on his staff

51

allowed to cover the war. The newsman's colleagues, angered by the ban, renewed their charges that Sherman was insane.

In January 1863, Lincoln had issued the Emancipation Proclamation, freeing all slaves that belonged to Confederate supporters. Sherman opposed the edict. He said that the masters had bought and paid for the slaves. The government had no right to take their property away. Besides, he added: "Where are they [the freed slaves] to get work? Who is to feed them, clothe them, and house them?"

During the winter months, Sherman and his troops tried to build a canal in Southern Louisiana. Grant hoped this canal would divert the Mississippi River and thus create a route for Union ships headed for Vicksburg. Sherman predicted that the project would be a failure because no one could predict the course of the Mississippi.

In April, nature achieved what Sherman could not. Spring rains and the natural flow of the river provided a safe route for Union ironclads, transports, and barges headed toward Vicksburg. Along the way, they engaged in several successful battles. By May 1, Sherman was ready to move toward Vicksburg by land. Grant asked him to bring 120 wagonloads of supplies, and Sherman was determined to do so.

He organized his regiments with strict attention to details. He insisted on a steady marching pace with little time out. Ever watchful for Confederate snipers, he taught his soldiers to dig trenches where they could rest safely each night. By day, they were continually alert for guerilla attacks. As much as possible, he maintained sanitary conditions in each camp. He opened roads, fought off snipers, and kept up the spirits of his men. When stricken with malaria, Sherman gave orders from an ambulance by the roadside.

Defender and Destroyer

This house served as Sherman's Chattanooga headquarters

Obtaining food was a major problem. Unable to transport fresh food, soldiers had to rely on farmers whose land they marched through. At first, Sherman insisted that the soldiers give receipts to all farmers whose food they took. Then he thought of an idea that might help persuade Confederates to join the Union side. He gave the farmers a choice. They could refuse to donate food. If they did, Sherman's troops would seize it. Or they could volunteer the food. If they did, the troops would issue a receipt promising payment after the war.

Sherman pushed his troops as fast as they could go. Confederate General John Pemberton, rushing to help defend Vicksburg, did the same. Pemberton won the race. On May 18, Pemberton stationed his 31,000 soldiers safely inside the Vicksburg encampment.

The next day, Sherman's and Grant's armies attacked Vicksburg. Although the Union troops fought with determination, they were, as Sherman said, "swept away as chaff thrown from the hand in a windy day."

Union soldiers retreated to the outskirts where they conducted a siege of the city. With dwindling supplies and no hope of reinforcements, General Pemberton surrendered on July 4, 1863.

Sherman wrote to Ellen: "I will renew hopes of getting a quiet home where we can grow up among our children."

He wanted to take part in the victorious march into Vicksburg. Instead he was ordered to begin a march to Jackson, Mississippi. His goal was to drive General Joseph Johnston out of that important stronghold.

This march demanded discipline. The temperature was in the 90s and above. Everywhere, dust lay ankle-deep. Drinking water was scarce. Frequent thunderstorms offered some relief until the air turned sticky and humid again. Sherman abandoned the idea of marching in columns. He allowed the men to walk loose and free. He frequently shared a meal—often coffee and a few chunks of hard bread—with his soldiers at their campfires. He said, "Soldiers have a right to see and know that the man who guides them is near enough to see with his own eyes ...."

As they traveled, Sherman's troops burned factories, railroad shops, and warehouses. They destroyed railroad tracks. Sherman took an active part in attacks against Confederates. Sherman no longer issued receipts for food and supplies taken by his soldiers. He said, "The destruction of corn or forage and provision in the enemy's country is a well-established law of war."

William Tecumesh Sherman Jr. (Willie)

W. T. Sherman

A pontoon and a pontoon bridge

By July 10, Sherman lay siege to Jackson. By July 17, General Johnston had fled.

Sherman and his troops made camp along the Big Black River to rest and wait out the steamy summer weather. Ellen and four of the children visited him there for six weeks. They settled in two big hospital tenets pitched together. Nine-year-old Willie was a favorite both with this father and with the soldiers. The soldiers "appointed" Willie a sergeant and taught him some of their drills.

In August Sherman was promoted to brigadier-general. He wrote to his foster father to assure him that the promotion was based on merit. Reporters praised his effectiveness. For the first time in many years, three aspects of Sherman's life showed promise: he was living with his family, he was secure in his job, and he was not dependent on his father-in-law.

Defender and Destroyer

Sherman received a Union proposal to enlist black soldiers. Northerners liked the idea because it strengthened the army. Abolitionists liked it because it gave the blacks an opportunity to fight against the people who had enslaved them. Sherman wanted no blacks among his troops. He explained, "With my opinions of Negroes and my experience, yea, prejudice, I cannot trust them yet." When blacks were sent to him, he used them only in the least significant jobs.

In September, Ellen headed back to Lancaster with the children. When they reached Memphis, they discovered that Willie had typhoid fever. He died twenty-four hours after he was taken to a hospital.

Sherman could say only: "... sleeping, waking, everywhere I see poor little Willie ... His loss is more to me than words can express, but I would not let it divert my mind from the duty I owe my country... On, on I must go to meet a soldier's fate ...."

Chapter Seven
HEADED FOR ATLANTA

Sherman started north on a three-hundred mile march to Chattanooga, Tennessee. His troops were needed to help Union armies there. Rain and mud slowed their march. Some of the men had no shoes. Soldiers carried all their belongings in blanket rolls slung over their shoulders. They were always hungry.

As they marched forward, men re-built destroyed railroad tracks in hopes of creating a supply line. Sherman told them, "The quicker you build the railroad, the quicker you'll get something to eat."

The troops faced minor skirmishes which they easily put down.

Sherman received word that the son of a Union major had been captured by Confederates. He had been tied to the tailboard of a wagon and driven north. Sherman gave the captors a choice. They could return the boy within 24 hours, or Sherman would keep four prominent Southerners tied to the tailboard of a wagon until the young man appeared. The captive was returned before the 24 hours were up.

Near Chattanooga, Sherman led 116 crudely made boats across the Tennessee River. As he had hoped, his men captured the Confederate sentries on the other side. Quietly, and very quickly, they built a pontoon bridge over 1300 feet long. By daylight, the rest of

Defender and Destroyer

the regiment, about 1000 men, had crossed over the bridge and were entrenched across the river.

Sherman believed that the Confederates had the advantage of strength and numbers at this point. Still, it was his duty to lead an advance against them. He gave his troops a message: they could follow orders without question, or they could expect to be sentenced to harsh labor or to death.

To Sherman's surprise, his troops forced the Confederates to flee. In the Battle of Missionary Ridge, the Union lost 5500 men, and the Confederates 3500.

Next, Sherman was ordered to Knoxville, Tennessee. There, General Ambrose Burnside's troops were under siege.

The march was difficult. Sherman's troops had used all their food supplies. They relied on foraging to keep from starving. Each soldier carried only one blanket or coat, not enough to keep out the November cold and wet. Along the way, Confederates sniped at them from all directions. Guerrillas sneaked ahead of the Union troops, burning bridges and blocking roads with felled trees and bushes. Sherman's men pushed on. Burnside was freed from siege in December.

In January 1864, Sherman made plans to destroy Confederate strongholds in the deep south. Among the most heavily populated areas, he targeted were: Meridian and the areas around Vicksburg and Jackson in Mississippi; Memphis in Tennessee; Shreveport and New Orleans in Louisiana; Mobile in Alabama; and Atlanta in Georgia.

Sherman organized carefully. He would need 35,000 horses, trained and ready to fight. The list of necessary supplies stretched endlessly—food, grain, hay, saddles, uniforms—1300 pounds of items every day. Soon after he left Chattanooga, he would have to depend on a single line of railroad track for new supplies. He seized freight cars, put together a portable railroad "kit" with repair tools, and trained hundreds of men to perform repairs. Some food was brought by wagon. Large guns were towed on wagons pulled by double teams of horses.

He warned reporters against publishing any of his movements. The reporters complained to President Lincoln. The president asked Sherman if he would loosen his restrictions. Sherman's answer was short and simple: "I will not change my order."

Before he started out, Sherman wrote to Tommy, ending his letter with "we must have peace, and that can only be by battle." He sent bouquets of flowers to his daughters. He suggested that they dry them and keep them as a reminder of the peace he was fighting for.

Near Dalton, Georgia, between Atlanta and Chattanooga, Sherman tried to seize control of the railroad. He pretended to attack and then speedily retreated, hoping to lure Confederates from his goal. The plan failed. Southern forces prevented the Union from taking control of that stretch of tracks.

Disappointed, but not frustrated, Sherman pushed south. At night, his men watched him walk back and forth in the light of the campfire. Some soldiers joked that he was so full of marching that he had to keep it up all night.

They laughed at him, but they also admired him. He had ready solutions for so many problems! He showed them how to string wires and insulators so that he was never far from a telegraph relay. He trained his bridge-builders well. Their work seemed almost like magic. They stretched canvas over boatlike frames, slid them into the water, strung them together, and laid down a board floor. One soldier

Defender and Destroyer

Sherman's troops built this 800-foot railroad bridge over the Chattahoochie River in four days

called Sherman "the champion bridge builder of the world."
Remembering problems with stragglers at Bull Run, Sherman trained his men to march double-quick. Because carrying tents and blankets slowed the pace, he allowed each soldier to carry only a knapsack and a canteen. He promised to punish any soldier who complained.

Some days, the troops could travel as far as sixteen miles. All along the way, the men had to stop to build and repair bridges and roads. They tore down barns and felled trees to make ramps over muddy areas. Before they left an area, they destroyed the bridges, filled the roads with trees and brush, and pulled up the ramps. If the Confederates tried to follow them, they would find it slow going.

In Meridian, Sherman's troops destroyed an arsenal and several storehouses. They found large quantities of food, arms, and clothing. "This is worth fifty millions to the government," Sherman said as he ordered everything destroyed. The troops also set fire to an arsenal and some hotels. They destroyed about a hundred miles of railroad track by burning the wooden ties, heating the rails red-hot and then twisting the iron around trees.

At first, Sherman paid little attention to praise from soldiers, other officers, and Union political leaders. As reports came in from the battles at Lookout Mountain, Missionary Ridge, Vicksburg, Chattanooga, Meridian, he was increasingly honored for both bravery and strategy. He wrote to Ellen: "I was not aware of the hold I had on the people ...." Finally he was confident: "... I know I stand very high with the army ..."

Southerners claimed that Sherman was hateful and cruel, that he destroyed property and harmed civilians. They spoke most bitterly about the fires he set, complaining about the "Sherman Torch." Sherman was unmoved. He believed that his duty was to paralyze the Confederacy.

Their homes and food supplies destroyed, many Southerners attached themselves to Sherman's troops. By the end of February, Sherman estimated that 5000 slaves and 1000 white refugees brought up the rear. Sherman allowed them to follow, but he did not allow them to share food or other supplies. The camp followers became foragers.

In March 1864, two and a half years after the emotional breakdown that almost ended his career, Sherman was named general-in-charge of all armies between the Allegheny mountains and the Mississippi River. He was responsible for tens of thousands of men scattered throughout the western states. He was the second most powerful military man in the United States. Only General Grant, now the commander of all Union forces, was his superior.

Although most Confederates didn't admit it, they were losing the war. Union ships blocked southern ports, keeping important supplies from both the military and civilian populations. Union troops, especially those under Sherman, had destroyed essential food and housing. Factories in the North continued to pour out food, arms, and equipment. The North had twice as many soldiers as the South. Sherman had a message for Confederates: "To those who submit to rightful law and authority, all gentleness and forbearance; but to the petulant and persistent secessionists, why, death is mercy and the quicker he or she is disposed of the better."

His men admired Sherman's courage and his ability to plan and carry out military strategies. They also liked him as a friend. They called him Uncle Billy, and chatted as they walked along the Mississippi Valley, side by side. Together, they walked through torrents of rain, sometimes sloshing in a foot of mud and water. Sherman wandered about the camp fires at night, making personal contact with as many of his soldiers as he could.

The men fought off snipers and made a few offensive assaults, but saved their equipment and their physical strength for the big attack on Atlanta, Georgia.

Atlanta was a highly desired prize with its network of railroads and important weapons factories. Just as meaningful to Sherman, Union control of Atlanta would show the Confederates that even their most beautiful cities could not escape punishment.

Along the way to Atlanta, Sherman seized control of private railroads. He closed the trains to civilians. He said the trains could not serve soldiers and civilians at the same time. To those civilians who demanded a seat on a train, he said, "Show me that your presence at the front is more valuable than two hundred pounds of powder."

The soldiers' worst problem was vermin, creeping "things" of every description that caused intolerable itching. Sometimes rubbing the bites with bacon rind helped. Salt water bathing would have helped, but salt was too scarce for such a use.

Sherman grew even more careless about his appearance. He wore a black felt hat over his long straggly hair, a faded and threadbare coat. His vest was stained with nicotine and ash from the endless cigars he smoked. He was probably the only officer who wore low shoes instead of boots.

As they moved along, Sherman's troops dug trenches and ditches to protect themselves at each camping place. They fired at snipers from these pits and then ducked. Before they left each encampment, they piled felled trees and brush all around to slow any enemies who might try to follow them.

Advance troops kept bridges and tracks clear so that freight cars could get through with supplies. When necessary, they built new bridges. One of Sherman's soldiers wrote that when an engine crossed a newly completed bridge, its whistle said "How-d-you-doo-oo-General-Sherman!".

As they moved south, more blacks asked for Sherman's protection. Many came with all their belongings—chests, quilts, ragged clothes. Sherman said he could not afford to feed the hundreds who wanted to tag along. He discouraged all followers except able-bodied men whom he hired at $10 a month as manual laborers.

Sherman heard little from home until July when he learned that he had a new son. Ellen's letters were not comforting. She wrote of her worries about the children, the high cost of living, and her own health problems.

Union soldiers seldom saw more than a few Confederates at once. The snipers dashed about from tree to tree and crouched behind bushes. Days and nights were filled the sounds of cannons firing and the whistle of shells.

On July 5, Sherman stood on a hill nine miles from Atlanta. With his field glasses, he watched Confederate soldiers as they dug trenches, set up guns, and prepared to fight the attackers.

Chapter Eight
DEFENDER AND DESTROYER?

Sherman moved across the Chattahoochee River on July 17, 1864. On the other side, he learned that Confederate General John Hood had replaced General Johnston. The new commander had a reputation for being bold and courageous. Sherman could expect trouble.

On July 20, Hood's troops came out from the city to attack. The Union forces forced them to retreat. On July 22, Hood struck again. This time, bullets bounced off the walls of Union headquarters, shells crashed all around Sherman's troops, and the roar of battle surrounded them. Sherman gave orders quickly. Soon Union and Confederate soldiers were fighting hand-to-hand with clubs, bayonets, and fists.

Sherman took charge of a cannon and sent some balls flying. A rifle bullet grazed his cheek. "Close shaving," he said. "We'll pay back that compliment."

At nightfall, General Hood's troops retreated into the city.

A dozen times a week, Sherman's and Hood's armies faced each other in the July heat. These frequent attacks kept both sides tense.

Food became scarce for Sherman's troops. One "meal" was a strip of raw pork sprinkled with brown sugar and eaten on hardtack.

Reporters who could get close enough commented that Sherman seemed too busy to eat or sleep. They described him as "wearing a gray flannel shirt, a faded old blue blouse, and trousers that he had worn since long before Chattanooga. He talked and smoked cigars incessantly, giving orders, dictating telegrams, bright and chipper."

By August, Sherman could hardly control his impatience to enter Atlanta. He and his men had marched over one hundred thirty miles through difficult terrain. They had been continually threatened and harassed by a stubborn enemy. It was time to score a victory.

Hood put an end to that impatience by retreating, leaving the city unprotected. On the night of September 2, Sherman began his move into the city. The streets were deserted. Many Atlantans had already fled; others remained inside their homes, fearful.

Sherman established guidelines for Atlantans. They could stay in Atlanta if they surrendered their loyalty to the South. If not, they would be forced to leave the city within two days. When Sherman heard complaints that he was cruel and barbaric, he answered, "...God will judge us in due time, and he will pronounce whether it be more humane to fight with a town full of women and the families of a brave people at our back, or to remove them in time to places of safety among their own friends and people."

Sherman pointed out that the situation would change when Confederates surrendered. "When peace does come, you may call on me for any thing. Then will I share with you the last cracker ...."

News of the evacuation order reached Ellen. She wrote to her husband: "I am charmed with your order expelling the inhabitants of Atlanta as it has always seemed to me preposterous to have our Government feeding so many of their people ..." Officials of the

Union War Department also stood behind Sherman's orders. Sherman received copies of newspapers several weeks old. He read with surprise that Democrats suggested that he was the perfect Presidential candidate. He had a quick answer: "If forced to choose between the penitentiary and the White House for four years ... I would say the penitentiary, thank you." He refused to say whether he preferred Lincoln or General George McClellan, who became the Democratic Party's candidate for President.

In November 1864, Sherman sent telegrams to newly-reelected President Lincoln and General Grant, telling them that he had a plan to bring the war to an end.

His plan focused on Confederate civilians as much as on soldiers. Civilians were contributing heavily to the war effort. They had set up networks to supply food and arms to their soldiers. They maintained strong guerilla and spy forces. Perhaps most important, they supported and encouraged their troops.

Sherman declared that the Union had to break this chain of support. They could do this by destroying Confederate homes, confiscating food and other supplies, and showing civilians the strength and determination of the Union military forces.

He proposed a march through Georgia to the seaport at Savannah, breaking Southern morale all along the way. He would make the Georgians beg to be free of the Confederacy. "I can make Georgia howl," he threatened. However, he added, he would continually hold out an olive branch. As soon as the South surrendered, he would offer a generous peace.

After his march to Savannah, Sherman planned to head back up north. He would attack, burn, and destroy everything he found along

Defender and Destroyer

Confederate General John Bell Hood

the way. The last step was to join his troops and General Grant's to force the surrender of General Robert E. Lee, a powerful Confederate general, somewhere near Richmond, Virginia, the capital of the Confederacy.

Both Grant and Lincoln gave Sherman permission to pursue his plan. They agreed that the plan would be most effective as a series of surprise attacks to the flanks of the Confederate army. Flanking attacks allowed Sherman's men to slip around the opposing troops and continue their progress while keeping casulties low.

Sherman told his men to prepare to march, but he refused to tell them where they were headed. He told them only that the march would be difficult and long, an advance into hostile territory.

He wrote to his children: "I am fighting now that you may live in peace. If I do lose my life, I know there will be some people still living who will take care of you."

On November 16, Sherman left the city with 55,000 men, 2500 light trucks, and 600 ambulances drawn by mules and horses. In fine spirits, the troops sang "Mine eyes have seen the glory of the coming of the Lord; He is trampling out the vintage where the grapes of wrath are stored ...."

Before they left Atlanta, the troops fired shells into homes, factories, and shops. Fire spread quickly. About one-third of the area was burned to ashes. One of Sherman's soldiers reported: "All the pictures and verbal descriptions of hell I have ever seen never gave me half so vivid an idea of it, as did this flame-wrapped city tonight."

Hate and terror spread across the South as Southerners learned of the fires. One paper called Sherman "the spirit of a thousand fiends centered in one."

Defender and Destroyer

Fortified union lines outside of Atlanta

Sherman's troops relax in captured Confederate fortifications

W. T. Sherman

As they advanced, Sherman's troops ate better than they had in a long time. Sherman said it was time for the Southerners to pay for the war. His troops could take all the food they needed from civilians along the way. Most days, after a few hours foraging, the soldiers returned with wagons bulging with sweet potatoes, sorghum, honey, molasses, ham, turkey, and chicken. In some places, they took so much food they left tons of it rotting on the ground behind them. They tied goats, cows, and mules to the backs of wagons. The goats and cows would furnish milk and meat; the mules would carry supplies when necessary. The soldiers also brought along farm wagons, buggies, and sulkies. Sometimes the men showed off in stolen finery—wigs, three-cornered hats, white trousers, and even women's clothes and jewelry. When asked, Sherman said that he opposed looting. But he did little to stop it. He knew that looting would terrorize civilians, and terror was what he wanted to create.

Newly freed slaves rushed to Sherman, calling him "the Angel of the Lord." Others called him a red-bearded Moses. Sherman made it clear that he could not feed them. He did accept some able-bodied blacks as workers, and he paid these men. Again, he refused Lincoln's request to enlist the blacks as soldiers. He was asked: Wasn't the Negro as good as a white man for stopping a bullet? "Yes," he answered, "and a sand-bag is better; but can a Negro do our skirmishing and picket duty? ...Can they improvise roads, bridges, sorties, flank movements, etc. like the white man? I say no."

Some whites also joined the march. These "bummers" were Union soldiers separated from their regiments, Confederate deserters, poor whites looking for a better life, drifters, and adventurers.

The 60,000 men marched ten to fifteen miles every day. On

Defender and Destroyer

Union troops destroying railroads outside of Atlanta before beginning the march to the sea.

W. T. Sherman

Thanksgiving Day they feasted in Milldegeville, Georgia. Unexpected company appeared. They were several Union soldiers who had escaped from the Confederate prison at Andersonville. These men were just barely strong enough to tell of the brutal treatment, lack of food, and filthy living conditions in prison. Their stories infuriated Sherman's troops who decided to "pay back" the Confederates with even more foraging and destruction.

Sherman learned that Governor Brown was urging Georgians to resist Sherman's advances: "Obstruct and destroy all the roads in Sherman's front, flank, and rear, and his army will soon starve in your midst. Assail the invader!" These announcements added to the rage of the Union soldiers. More reasons to punish Southerners.

For thirty-three days, the troops marched. Neither Confederate nor Union reporters knew where Sherman might encamp next. They could always tell where he had been from the stories of destruction. But they could only guess where he would turn up next. Even President Lincoln did not know: "I can know the hole he went in at, but I can't tell you what hole he will come out of."

Along the way, one of Sherman's lieutenant's stepped on a Confederate-planted mine. He lost his foot. Sherman broke accepted rules of warfare. He forced Confederate prisoners of war to search the area for other mines.

As he approached Savannah, Sherman learned that Confederate General William Hardee, commander of Savannah, had burned the thousand-foot bridge across the Ogeechee River. Sherman ordered his men to dismantle houses and fell trees to collect wood to rebuild the bridge. On December 13, he marched his troops across that bridge, ready for the charge. In a fifteen-minute flurry of flags, cannon balls,

Defender and Destroyer

Sherman looking over recently defeated Atlanta

rockets, and rifle bullets, the Union soldiers forced the Confederates to retreat from Fort McAlister, fifteen miles out of Savannah.

Sherman sent a note to Hardee, giving him a choice. If Hardee ordered both soldiers and civilians to obey Sherman, the Union general would treat him kindly. If he did not issue the order Sherman said, "I shall make little effort to restrain my army—burning to avenge the national wrong ..."

Hardee refused to surrender.

Sherman marched into Savannah on December 21. The inhabitants surrendered without a fight. Hardee had fled. As in Atlanta, Sherman captured the city without killing the commander. Sherman knew he would probably have to fight Hardee at some time, but he was content that he had met his goal for the present. He was in charge of Savannah. He wrote to his children: "Of course I must fight when the time comes, but wherever a result can be accomplished without Battle I prefer it." Sherman had changed since his first days in the military when he was eager to take part in fighting.

On December 22, Sherman sent President Lincoln a telegram: "I beg to present you as a Christmas gift, the city of Savannah, with one hundred and fifty heavy guns and plenty of ammunition, also about twenty-five thousand bales of cotton." Lincoln returned a message beginning with: "... Many many thanks for your Christmas gift—the capture of Savannah ..."

Sherman was thrilled when he learned that Thomas Ewing told his colleagues he was proud of his stepson. Sherman wrote to him: "I would rather please and gratify you than all the world beside."

Sherman learned from a newspaper that Charles Ewing Sherman, a son he had never seen, had died. He wrote to John: "... were it not

Defender and Destroyer

This scene of destruction resulted from Confederate General Hood blowing up his own supply train

W. T. Sherman

A section of Atlanta after Sherman's troops left for Savannah

for General Grant's confidence in me, I should insist upon a little rest. As it is I must go on."

Sherman had accomplished a lot for the Union. His troops had destroyed Georgia as a possible source of supplies for Confederate armies. Georgian civilians were depressed, lacking both energy and means to support their cause. Sherman had accomplished this with comparatively little loss of Union soldiers.

Now he set out to repair some of the damage. Savannah was a beautiful city with large yards around brick and frame houses and handsome shade trees. Stores and warehouses lined a street facing the sea. But the siege had damaged property and spirits. Sherman reorganized the police force, opened the schools, and helped store owners to establish business again. He declared, "I doubt if Savannah, either before or since, has had a better government than during our stay."

Sherman began immediate preparations to continue his plan to end the war. He wrote to his family that the next campaign would be 10 times more difficult, 10 times more important, and just as mysterious as the march to the sea. He said that he thought his chances of being killed were about 50-50. He warned them not to expect news of him. He ordered that any journalist who seemed to have information about his itinerary should be imprisoned until Sherman had completed his route. He said he would "dive again beneath the surface to turn up again in some mysterious place."

Chapter Nine
THE SMOKY MARCH

Confederate military leaders tried to guess Sherman's route. They knew he was headed north. They were sure he would not cross the Whippy Swamp in southern South Carolina. General Johnston said, "My engineers reported that it was absolutely impossible for an army to march across lower portions of the State in winter."

Johnston's engineer did not know what Sherman knew. He had lived in the Florida swamps, and he had enjoyed hunting trips in southern creeks, bayous and swamps. Many of his men were westerners, used to a pioneer's life. They knew how to split saplings to lay down for wagon crossings. They had experience wading across icy creeks with clothes piled on their heads so they would have something warm and dry to wear on the other side. They knew how to withstand rain, cold, physical exertion. Whippy Swamp would be a challenge, but not an obstacle.

In January 1865, Sherman started up the coast, headed for Columbia, South Carolina, the state capitol. To confuse the Confederates, he sent some troops to Charleston and some to Atlanta. All troops were given orders to burn, loot, and destroy property, "to whip the rebels, to humble their pride, to follow them to their inmost recesses, and make them fear and dread us. Fear is the beginning of wisdom."

It rained more than half of the first forty-five days of the march to Columbia. The men, including Sherman, often slept in trees, preferring the heights to sodden ground. Sherman eliminated drills and inspections that would have further exhausted and exasperated the men. He saw no reason to increase their problems.

After Columbia fell in February, the men set fire to over a thousand homes. They piled thousands of bales of cotton in the streets to be torched. They lit fires on railroad cars, in supply depots, in acres of pine trees, public buildings, and sometimes throughout entire towns. By now the campaign had been nicknamed The Smoky March. The troops were particularly eager to destroy property in South Carolina, the state where citizens had fired the first shot of the war. Sherman knew that the first men to enter the city would celebrate by destroying, burning, and looting. He might have issued orders against such behavior, but he didn't.

Sherman's men raged around the town with lighted torches, setting fires at will. Some raided liquor stores, and they celebrated with more than a few drinks.

By morning, 1300 houses were burned, leaving 7,000 people homeless. Rumors flew. Some said that Sherman's men were completely responsible. Others said that the bummers had caused most of the damage. Still others said that slaves had set the fires. Others said that Columbians had started the fires themselves, not wanting to leave spoils of war to the Union.

The next day, Sherman did what he could for suffering families. He gave them 500 cattle to ease their food shortage. He sent his personal allotment of rations to needy families. He said, "Though I never ordered it and never wished it, I have never shed many tears over the event, because I believe it hastened what we all fought for, the end of the war."

Furious, committee of citizens asked Sherman why he had allowed his troops to burn the city. He answered, "I did not burn your town, nor did my army. Your brothers, sons, husbands, and fathers set fire to every city, town, and village in the land when they fired on Fort Sumter. That fire kindled then and there by them has been burning ever since, and reached your houses last night."

The victorious army continued moving north. By the time Sherman crossed the state boundary into North Carolina, he had picked up about 25,000 "extra" marchers. These were whites who had fled from the destruction of their cities and blacks who had escaped from their masters.

North Carolina had been the last state of the Confederacy to secede. Sherman wanted to honor their reluctance by treating them more gently than he had the South Carolinians. He hoped to win them over to the Union side. He told his officers to "fan the flame of discord already subsisting between them and their proud cousins of South Carolina...."

As they marched through turpentine forests, Sherman's troops touched burning matches to knots of sap. Sparks became fires which spread quickly. The air became so thick with smoke that no one could see the sky for miles.

Confederate General Johnston's troops initiated sniper attacks on Sherman's troops. When the attacks grew to be skirmishes, Sherman pulled his troops away. He wanted to save all his strength for the

Defender and Destroyer

offensive he expected to come at Goldsboro, North Carolina, a major railroad center.

Sherman's men had traveled over 425 miles of swamp, forest, field, and stream. More than half of the soldiers were shoeless; some walked on blood-stained wrappings of old blankets. Some wore trousers so torn that their bare legs showed. All were physically exhausted. Still, they were proud of themselves and of their leader. They knew that the scene was set for victory. Sherman was pleased, too. Again, he had advanced the Union Army closer to victory without engaging in a major battle.

Johnston's troops retreated from Goldsboro, leaving Sherman to enter freely on March 23. On that day 80,000 cheering Union soldiers marched into the city.

Sherman met with General Grant and President Lincoln. The generals discussed strategy for the remaining battles—Grant against Lee in Virginia and Sherman against Johnston in North Carolina. Lincoln talked of the peace to come. They all agreed that the biggest problem would be to restore state and local governments to efficient operation.

Sherman had grown to respect Lincoln during the war years. "Of all the men I ever met, he seemed to possess more of the elements of greatness, combined with goodness, than any other."

On April 9, Lee surrendered to Grant at Appomattox Courthouse in Virginia. Sherman's troops rejoiced, bands played "Yankee Doodle" and "Home Sweet Home." The war was not over, but Union confidence was high.

On April 12, Sherman announced to his men "Glory to God and our country and all honor to our comrades in arms ...." They set out to find and attack Johnston's army.

On April 14, General Johnston and CSA President Davis wrote to Sherman. They asked for a meeting to arrange an armistice.

Sherman agreed: "I really desire to save the people of North Carolina the damage they would sustain by the march of this army." Johnston rushed back a reply setting a meeting on the 17th at Durham Station, North Carolina, a site between the two camps.

On his way to the meeting on the 17th, Sherman received astounding news. President Lincoln had been assassinated. After the shock of grief and loss lessened, Sherman realized that this news could set off riots and demonstrations throughout the Union. For the length of the 26-mile train trip, Sherman kept his worries to himself as he and his men talked cheerfully about the coming surrender.

At the station, a Union soldier with a white flag rode ahead of Sherman and his aides. About 5 miles out, they met a Confederate soldier with a white flag riding ahead of Johnston. The two generals shook hands. Then they went into a nearby farm house. Once the two men were alone, Sherman gave Johnston the news about Lincoln.

Both generals worried that Confederates might be blamed for the murder. They would do what they could do to keep down accusations and rumors. Meanwhile, they must discuss the armistice. Surely, this is what Lincoln would have wanted.

Johnston wanted to talk about more than a cease-fire for his own troops. He wanted to talk about a cease-fire for the whole Confederate army. Sherman was ready to go along with that. He believed the Southerners had been punished enough. They parted with good feelings about each other, promising to meet again after Johnston obtained permission to negotiate for all Confederate armies.

Defender and Destroyer

Confederate General Joseph E. Johnston

Back in camp, Sherman issued a carefully worded bulletin announcing the assassination. He emphasized that the Confederacy had nothing to do with the crime. He met tears and anger, but no reaction to threaten the fragile armistice negotiations.

The next day Sherman and Johnston met again. Johnston had permission to complete the armistice for all Southern soldiers. He asked for assurance that surrendering Confederates would be treated well. Sherman agreed. He also agreed that the Union would recognize the governments of Southern states and that no Southerner would be punished as long as he obeyed Union laws. Satisfied, Sherman sent a report to President Andrew Johnson, successor to Lincoln.

On April 24, Secretary of War Stanton sent an angry message to Sherman. The armistice agreement was decidedly not acceptable. Sherman had overstepped his bounds. He had been ordered only to stop hostilities. He had no right to discuss guarantees about treatment, recognition of state governments, or punishment for war crimes. Stanton demanded that Sherman write a new armistice agreement which considered the single topic of unconditional surrender.

An obedient soldier, Sherman wrote to Stanton, apologizing for his references to civic matters. On April 26, Sherman and Johnston signed an unconditional surrender. Then Sherman returned to his camp, where he announced to anyone who would listen: "I believe that the General Government of the United States has made a mistake but that is none of my business; mine is a different task ..." Sadness ran deep inside him. He had promised Southerners over and over that they would not be punished when they stopped fighting against the Union. Now these promises were to be broken.

A few days later, Sherman caught up with newspaper reports

covering events of the preceding week. He was enraged to learn that Stanton had criticized him widely in the press. Stanton even hinted that CSA President Davis was going to pay off Sherman for proposing such easy terms. He declared that the conditions of the armistice insured that the South would begin fighting again as soon as the Union armies disbanded. Headlines announced: "Sherman has fatally blundered" and "Sherman was completely over-reached and outwitted by Joe Johnston."

Once again, Sherman was publicly being called a traitor. In vain, he explained that punishing the South would only create more problems, that it would be "like slashing away at the crew of a sinking ship." In a rage, he lashed out at Stanton. He called the Secretary of War a "mean, scheming, vindictive politician." Some of his troops demonstrated to show their faith in Sherman. Sherman appreciated the gesture, but still he vowed revenge.

On top of all this, Sherman learned that on April 22, General Halleck had wired Union officers, ordering them to disregard the truce that Sherman was negotiating. He told them to ignore any orders from Sherman.

Although depressed, Sherman carried out his assigned duties. As others worked out final details of surrender, Sherman headed for Savannah to supervise distribution of food and supplies to troops. From Savannah, Sherman spread food and good will throughout the state. He ordered his men to distribute corn, meal, and flour to needy families.

On May 10, Jefferson Davis, who had fled Richmond, was captured. Rumors said that soldiers found him disguised in his wife's raincoat and shawl. Sixteen days later, all southern resistance ended when Confederate General Kirby Smith surrendered to General Edward Canby at New Orleans.

The conflict between Sherman and Stanton continued to boil. President Andrew Johnson, General Grant, and the Cabinet (except Stanton) tried to calm Sherman down. They praised him for his military victories. They explained that they knew that communications problems, not self-interest, had created the problems with the first armistice. They asked Sherman to make peace with Stanton. He refused. He planned to get his revenge at the Conduct of the War investigations.

At an investigation session on May 22, Sherman's accusers said that he had betrayed his country when he arranged the first armistice with Johnston. Sherman answered that he believed that he was following Lincoln's wishes on the matter.

Investigators did not know whom to believe. The session ended with unanswered questions. The fact that questions were unanswered left suspicion against Sherman in the minds of many. Even his wife qualified her respect for him, saying "... however much I differ from you..."

On May 24, Sherman led his troops in a victory march in front of the White House where President Johnson, Cabinet members, and other dignitaries waited to salute them. Ellen and eight-year-old Tommy sat beside the dignitaries on wooden bleachers. Sherman's horse was covered with floral wreaths and garlands.

Spectators climbed trees, crowded together on rooftops, and lined each side of Pennsylvania Avenue, waving handkerchiefs and black silk hats. They cheered, "Hail to the Western Heroes" and "Hail, Champions." Bands blared "The Star Spangled Banner."

As he passed the dignitaries' stand, Sherman spun in his saddle to inspect his men. Every one was in perfect lock-step order, proud and precise. Sherman whipped out his sword and saluted the President. A reporter wrote: "The whole assemblage raised and waved and shouted as if he had been the personal friend of each and every one of them ... " Sherman wrote later, "I believe it was the happiest and most satisfactory moment of my life."

After leaving the parade, Sherman went to the White House. He embraced Ellen and Tommy. He shook hands with Johnson and Grant. Without a word, he ignored Stanton's outstretched hand.

After that day, Sherman had only one obligation. That was to keep his troops in order until they could be officially released.

On May 30, he gave a farewell address to his men. He warned against future armed conflict: "I think that the interest of the whole country demands that when troubles arise, they should be determined by the courts of law and not by the force of the musket." He ended: "Our work is done... you have been good soldiers ... you will make good citizens."

After four years of conflict, the Civil War left 600,000 men dead. Thousands more were wounded. Hundreds of thousands of families had to learn to live without loved ones. Land, buildings, and railroads were destroyed throughout the South. The assassination of Lincoln left deep scars and fears. The problems of emancipation had not been faced.

Citizens were not ready to put the war behind them. Sherman was showered with invitations to speak. Almost everywhere, he found both affection and respect. He avoided meetings where he suspected conflict with his ideas. He stayed away from politics. He wrote to

Grant: "My opinion is, the country is being doctored to death, and if President and Congress would go to sleep like Rip Van Winkle, the country would go on under natural influences and recover far faster than under their joint and several treatment." Crowds cheered as he told them: "We have the best country on earth. Our history in the past is beautiful, and her future is in our keeping ... For fifty years to come, at least, I never want to hear a word about war in America."

Sherman enjoyed the crowds. A reporter wrote that he "amused himself and everybody else by his frolicsome snatching of kisses from young women...."

Chapter Ten
"FAITHFUL AND HONORABLE"

President Johnson wanted to replace the controversial Stanton. In January 1866, he asked Sherman to take over as Secretary of War. Sherman refused: "For eleven years I have been tossed about so much that I really do want to rest, study, and make the acquaintance of my family ..."

Johnson found another task for him. He asked Sherman to help him to fight against Congressional representatives who believed that blacks should be allowed to vote without question. Johnson believed that blacks should earn that right. The president hoped that Sherman's popularity as a war hero would encourage lawmakers to agree with him. Sherman refused.

Next Johnson asked for Sherman's help with a problem in the West. Pioneers were building railroads, homes, and trading posts on land the Indians believed was theirs. The United States government supported the pioneers. They set aside plots of land, and they required that Indians stay on these reservations. The Indians resisted. Sherman's job, as a member of the Indian Commission, was to enforce the requirement and to ensure that the Indians did not retaliate.

This was an ideal assignment for Sherman. He appreciated the task of enforcing laws. He loved the idea of working in the open air of the Great Plains.

Sherman's family joined him in his St. Louis headquarters. For the first time in many years, they settled down together for an indefinite period of time. In January, 1867, Philemon Tecumseh was born. "I think there is no doubt we can raise this young chap," Sherman said. "And I hope this completes the family."

Sherman was genuinely interested in his children. He hoped the boys would go into law. He wanted his daughters to be "educated, cultivated women, fitted for faithful wives and mothers." He often took them riding. Sometimes they went to the theater, circus, and minstrel shows. Sometimes the family read aloud together, Shakespeare, modern authors, and plays. Ellen described summer nights on the lawn outside their home, "... the old folks reading the papers, the young people playing croquet, the children frisking about, the hummingbirds dipping into the flowers, and the canary singing overhead."

As he had years before with the Seminoles, Sherman told the Navahoes, Cheyennes, Ogallalas, and other tribes that they would be treated well as long as they obeyed. He explained: "We will be kind to you if you keep the peace, but if you won't listen to reason we are ordered to make war upon you." He justified use of force against the Indians: "We cannot allow the Indians to roam at large ... because if they do there will surely be collision and bloodshed ... Moral force is not strong enough ... The Indians hardly understand it."

In 1866, Sioux Indians killed all eighty members of a Federal force. Sherman reacted quickly. He commanded his troops to punish "until at least ten Indians are killed for each white life lost."

Defender and Destroyer

Sherman also supervised the completion of the transcontinental railroad that would stretch from California to Kansas. Railroads had been an important part of Sherman's life before. As a banker in California, he had invested in them. As a military man, he had relied on them. He predicted that railroads could become important to military security again. He found no sympathy with Indians who objected to the idea of noisy smoky monsters running through their wide open lands.

Sherman supervised the laying of track. Some of his soldiers had served with him a few years earlier, when he had supervised the destruction of track in the South. Now they joked about the change of jobs.

Sherman enjoyed the life of a railroad overseer. He slept in a blanket roll, boiled his coffee on a campfire made from buffalo chips, and spent hours in the open. A general who worked with him described him: "... he acted like a boy turned loose—threw off reserve—asked 1000 questions of everybody—never at a loss for a story or joke—a comic twinkle in his eye ...." The highest station on the line, a depot in the Rocky Mountains, was named Sherman to honor his accomplishments in the building of the railroad.

Sherman was in Washington on May 10, 1869 when the transcontinental tracks were joined. Over telegraph wires, he received the message that the last spike was driven at Promontory Point in Utah, 2500 miles west of the Atlantic, 790 miles east of the Pacific.

Sherman moved up to Grant's position as general-in-chief of the army when Grant became President in 1869. Immediately he became involved in politics, red tape, bureaucracy, and personal conflicts. A Congressional representative complained publicly that Sherman demanded too much compensation for travel and entertainment. Sherman defended his expenditures. Nevertheless, Congress voted to cut his salary from $18,000 to $12,000. His pride wounded, Sherman considered resigning from the army.

Before he could make the move, he was invited on a good will tour of Europe with a military friend, Admiral Alden. Sherman quickly accepted. Although he traveled as a private citizen, several heads of state welcomed him. He enjoyed visits with leaders in France, Italy, Turkey, and Russia. He enjoyed the fanfare, but he was delighted to come back home after ten months. "I like American scenery better than any," he admitted.

On his return, he discovered that some of his duties had been assigned to other military leaders. Enraged, he said that was the last insult he would accept from Washington. He asked permission to move his staff to St. Louis, far from Washington politicians. He would retire soon, he said, and he saw no benefit to putting up with Congressional scolding and harassing for his last few months. President Chester Arthur agreed. The Sherman family moved to St. Louis where grateful citizens had bought a house for him.

During the 1870s and 80s, Sherman was seen and heard by more people than any other American speaker. He particularly appreciated veterans' reunions, and he frequently marched with them. He praised their dedication to their country, but repeated: "I think we understand what military fame is—to be killed on the field of battle and have our names spelled wrong in the newspapers." Sherman never asked for speaking fees or appeared where admission was charged.

Now that Sherman had fewer military duties, he worked on his memoirs. He wrote the first seven chapters about his life up to 1861.

Sherman in 1869, while serving in the west

W. T. Sherman

The rest of the twenty-four chapters focused on the war. He wrote about strategies, battles and problems. He included letters he wrote himself, letters from other military leaders, and official battle reports and statistics. In March, 1875, D. Appleton Company, publishers, accepted the manuscript.

The eight hundred-page book was published in two volumes, handsome editions in blue covers with gold lettering. The book became a best seller.

Some reviewers said that Sherman flattered himself in the book. Criticism of the book opened up new criticism of Sherman. Southerners were impatient with their slow recovery from the war. They put some of the blame on Sherman who, they said, created more destruction than was necessary or appropriate. Both Northerners and Southerners criticized him for his opposition to the 15th Amendment which gave blacks the right to vote.

Sherman wrote dozens of magazine articles, defending his actions and ideas. He was sure he was right.

In 1876, Republican leaders asked him to run for President. No, no, and no again, he replied. Republican candidate Rutherford B. Hayes eventually defeated Democrat Samuel Tilden in the closest Presidential election ever.

Sherman described his army duties as "routine matters," of little interest to anyone. Nevertheless, he obeyed orders to approve and record movements of troops, leaves of absence, reports, and the like. Sherman found excitement outside of his work. He was a popular guest in Washington D.C. society and in other cities as well. He spoke at West Point graduation ceremonies. He received honorary degrees from Dartmouth, Yale, and Princeton.

In 1879, Sherman took a tour through the South. He wanted to inspect military installations. Perhaps even more important, he wanted to know how Southerners felt about him. When he returned from the trip, he reported: "... the people high and low received me with absolute cordiality and friendship ...."

Sherman spent the next few years in a small office in his home. He maintained privacy with a large sign on the door that said "General Sherman's Office." He entertained veterans, read and wrote letters, and re-read his favorite novels by Burns, Scott, and Dickens. Ellen also had her own small office. A devout Catholic, she spent her time working on religious causes and charities.

In November 1883, Sherman was sixty-four, close to the mandatory retirement age for soldiers. Without complaining, Sherman retired. Once again, he was urged to run for President in 1884, and again, he refused.

He had to refuse again when he received a telegram from the Republican convention, telling him that he would be nominated. He telegraphed back, "Please decline any nomination for me in language strong but courteous."

He received another telegram: "Your name is the only one we can agree upon, you will have to put aside your prejudices and accept the Presidency."

He replied, "I will not accept if nominated and will not serve if elected."

If Sherman had accepted all his invitations to speak, he would have been on stage at least once a day. Outwardly, he protested and complained, but inside, he was thrilled with the attention. After years of dependence on Ewing, failures at jobs, disgrace as a military man, and scorn from political leaders, Sherman was popular and self-confident.

Ellen complained frequently about her health—breathing problems, indigestion, emotional disturbances, and lack of energy. When Sherman suggested that she might be more comfortable in a new home in New York City, she agreed. They moved into a brownstone near Central Park in September, 1888. The move did not help. Ellen died from heart problems a few months later. In his grief, Sherman murmured, "Wait for me, Ellen, no one ever loved you as I love you."

Close to seventy years old, Sherman grew physically weak. He planned his funeral with a simple military ceremony. For a monument, he wanted no tomb or vault, just a stone engraved with the insignias of armies he had commanded. His grave was to be placed beside Ellen's and their sons Willie and Charles. He asked that the words "Faithful and Honorable" be chiseled on his gravestone.

On February 14, 1891, General Sherman died of complications of pneumonia and a stroke. His body lay in state in their New York City home. He wore his general's uniform with the yellow sash across his chest. His soldier's cap and sword lay beside him.

His old adversary General Johnston was a pall-bearer. As he stood outside in a brisk wind, someone suggested that he should not bare his head because he had not yet recovered from a recent illness. Johnston answered, "If I were in his place and he were standing in mine, he would not put on his hat." Five weeks later Johnston died.

Thousands jammed the streets and sidewalks to see the hearse that took Sherman's body to the funeral train that would travel to St. Louis. Crowds marched slowly down the street beside and behind the hearse. Fifes sang, drums rolled, and flags waved.

Defender and Destroyer

General William T. Sherman retired as his country's most respected military leader

At train stops along the way to St. Louis, crowds gathered to pay their last respects.

In St. Louis, the coffin was lowered into the ground. Veterans fired three musket blasts. A bugle played taps.

An editor at the *Atlanta Constitution* wrote: "When all is said that can be said, the fact looms up that this man was one of the greatest soldiers of the age ... But when the business of war was over ... he showed a softer side, and men and women, even among his former foes, found him a very lovable man."

TIMELINE

1820 — Born in Lancaster, Ohio.
1829 — Adopted by Thomas Ewing.
1836 — Enters West Point.
1840 — Graduates from West Point. Commissioned as Second Lieutenant in the U.S. Army.
1850 — Marries Ellen Ewing.
1853 — Resigns from the army. Begins a career as a banker.
1859 — Becomes Superintendent of the Louisiana Military Seminary.
1861 — Returns to Ohio and re-enters U. S. Army. Fights at Bull Run. Controversy erupts over his "sanity."
1862 — Fights at Shiloh under Grant.
1863 — Assists Grant in the Vicksburg Campaign.
1862 — Successfully battles his way from Chattanooga to Atlanta. Takes Atlanta in September, Savannah in December.
1865 — Accepts General Joseph Johnston's surrender in North Carolina. Controversy erupts over the surrender terms.
1866 — Placed in charge of the Indian Wars.
1869 — Appointed General-in-Chief of the Army.
1883 — Retires from the army.
1891 — Dies in New York City.

Notes

CHAPTER ONE

p. 9 "If the people howl . . ." Lewis, Lloyd. *Sherman: Fighting Prophet*. New York: Harcourt, Brace and Co., 1932, p. 415.

p. 11 "You must give me . . ." Lewis, op. cit., p. 32.

p. 13 "I felt the beauty . . ." Merrill, James. *William Tecumseh Sherman*. Chicago: Rand McNally & Co., 1971, p. 30.

p. 14 "I can't do that . . ." Lewis, op. cit., p.63.

p. 14 "I would be the last . . ." Merrill, op. cit., p. 33.

CHAPTER TWO

p. 19 "I have felt tempted . . ." Lewis, op. cit., p. 77.

p. 22 "My household expenses . . ." Merrill, op. cit., p.87.

CHAPTER THREE

p. 23 "Wherever I go . . ." Merrill, op. cit., p. 77.

p. 30 "on the ground . . ." Coburn, Mark. *Terrible Innocence: General Sherman at War*. New York: Hippocrene Books, p. 33.

p. 31 "I would not if I could . . ." Merrill, op. cit., p. 136.

p. 32 "Only a brother . . ." Hart, B. H. Liddell. *Sherman: Solider, Realist, American*. New York: Frederick Praeger, 1958, p. 56.

CHAPTER FOUR

p. 33 "If Louisiana withdraws . . ." Lewis, op. cit., p. 143.

p. 34 "You are all here . . ." Marszalek, John. *Sherman: A Solider's Passion for Order*. New York: The Free Press, 1993, p.139.

p. 34 "The United States seems . . ." Lewis, op. cit., p. 136.

p. 34 "Oh, well, I guess we'll manage . . ." Hart, op. cit., p. 67.

p. 36 "The North just don't care . . ." Merrill, op. cit., p. 155.

p. 36 ". . . a long war. . ." Hart, op. cit., p. 74.

p. 37 ". . . a tall gaunt form . . ." Marszalek, op. cit., p. 147.

p. 38 "Tell Colonel Sherman . . ." Lewis, op. cit., p. 170.

p. 39 "They became clamorous . . ." Merrill, op. cit., p. 167.

CHAPTER FIVE

p. 41 ". . . a general with such a hat . . ." Hart, op. cit., p. 101.

p. 41 ". . . on business just as important . . ." Sherman, William. *Memoirs of General William T. Sherman*. Bloomington: Indiana University Press, 1957, p. 201.

p. 41 "Great God! . . ." Sherman, op. cit., p. 203.

p. 41 "Our force here is out . . ." Sherman, op. cit., p. 205.

p. 42 ". . .absolutely crazy" Coburn, op. cit., p. 40.

p. 42 "His eye had a half-wild expression." Merrill, op. cit., p. 184.

p. 42 "General William T. Sherman, Insane." Coburn, op. cit., p. 41.

p. 43 ". . . physical and mental system is so completely broken . . ." Lewis, op. cit., p. 200.

p. 43 "I do think . . ." Merrill, op. cit., p. 189.

p. 44 "We are in great danger . . ." Lewis, op. cit., p. 214.

p. 47 "It is the unanimous opinion . . ." Hart, op. cit., p. 133.

p. 47 "The scenes on this field . . ." Coburn, Mark. *Terrible Innocence: General Sherman at War*. New York: Hippocrene Books, 1993, p. 44.

p. 47 "Built narrow and almost effeminate . . ." Lewis, op. cit., p. 233.

CHAPTER SIX

p. 48 "The military for the time being . . ." Marszalek, op. cit., p. 191.
p. 49 "You boys had better . . ." Marszalek, op. cit., p. 198.
p. 50 "Indeed I wish . . ." Hart, op. cit., p. 179.
p. 52 "Where are they to get work?" Marszalek, op. cit., p. 193.
p. 54 ". . . swept away as chaff . . ." Marszalek, op. cit., p. 226.
p. 54 "I will renew hopes . . ." Lewis, op. cit., p. 292.
p. 54 "Soldiers have a right . . ." Hart, op. cit., p. 168.
p. 56 "The destruction of corn . . ." Marszalek, p. 223.
p. 57 "With my opinions . . ." Lewis, op. cit., p. 303.
p. 57 ". . . sleeping, waking, everywhere . . ." Hart, op. cit., p. 201.

CHAPTER SEVEN

p. 58 "The quicker you build . . ." Lewis, op. cit., p. 314.
p. 60 "I will not change . . ." Marszalek, op. cit., p. 264.
p. 60 "We must have peace . . ." Marszalek, op. cit., p. 247.
p. 62 "the champion bridge builder. . ." Lewis, op. cit., p. 360.
p. 62 "This is worth fifty millions . . ." Lewis, op. cit., p. 333.
p. 62 "I was not aware . . ." Hart, op. cit., p. 299.
p. 63 "To those who submit . . ." Lewis, op. cit., p. 335.
p. 64 "Show me that your presence . . ." Merrill, op. cit., p. 245.
p. 65 "How-do-you-doo-oo-General Sherman." Lewis, op. cit., p. 373.

CHAPTER EIGHT

p. 66 "Close shaving . . ." Lewis, op. cit., p. 386.
p. 67 ". . . wearing a gray flannel shirt . . ." Lewis, op. cit., p. 401.
p. 67 "God will judge us . . ." Lewis, op. cit., p. 417.
p. 67 "When peace does come . . ." Lewis, op. cit., p. 416.

Defender and Destroyer

p. 67 "I am charmed . . ." Marszalek, op. cit., p. 286.
p. 68 "If forced to choose . . ." Lewis, op. cit., p. 411.
p. 68 "I can make Georgia howl . . ." Lewis, op. cit., p. 429.
p. 70 "I am fighting now . . ." Merrill, op. cit., p. 268.
p. 70 "All the pictures and verbal description . . ." Merrill, op. cit., p. 267.
p. 72 "Yes, and a sand bag is better . . ." Lewis, op. cit., p. 394.
p. 74 "Obstruct and destroy . . ." Lewis, op. cit., p. 449.
p. 74 "I can know the hole . . ." Lewis, op. cit., p. 458.
p. 76 "I shall make little effort . . ." Sherman, op. cit., p. 211.
p. 76 "Of course I must fight . . ." Marszalek, op. cit., p. 309.
p. 76 "I beg to present to you . . ." Lewis, op. cit., p. 470.
p. 76 "I would rather please . . ." Marszalek, op. cit., p. 311.
p. 76 ". . . were it not for General Grant's . . ." Lewis, op. cit., p. 476.
p. 79 "I doubt if Savannah . . ." Sherman, op. cit., p. 236.
p. 79 ". . . dive again beneath the surface . . ." Lewis, op. cit., p. 484.

CHAPTER NINE
p. 80 "My engineers reported . . ." Lewis, op. cit., p. 484.
p. 80 ". . . to whip the rebels, . . ." Lewis, op. cit., p. 488.
p. 82 "Though I never ordered it . . ." Merrill, op. cit., p. 283.
p. 82 "I did not burn your town . . ." Marszalek, op. cit., p. 509.
p. 82 ". . . fan the flame of discord . . ." Lewis, op. cit., p. 509.
p. 83 "Of all the men I ever met, . . ." Lewis, op. cit., p. 526.
p. 83 "Glory to God . . ." Marszalek, op. cit., p. 339.
p. 84 "I really desire . . ." Lewis, op. cit., p. 533.
p. 86 "I believe that the General Government . . ." Lewis, op. cit., p. 556.
p. 87 ". . . like slashing away . . ." Lewis, op. cit., p. 558.
p. 88 "However much I differ . . ." Lewis, op. cit., p. 572.

p. 89 "The whole assemblage raised . . ." Lewis, op. cit., p. 575.
p. 89 "I think that the interest . . ." Lewis, op. cit., p. 585.
p. 89 "My opinion is, the country . . ." Lewis, op. cit., p. 593.
"p. 90 . . . amused himself and everybody else . . ." Lewis, op. cit., p. 583.

CHAPTER TEN

p. 91 "For eleven years . . ." Lewis, op. cit., p. 591.
p. 92 ". . . the old folks reading the papers . . ." Marszalek, op. cit., p. 405.
p. 92 "We will be kind . . ." Lewis, op. cit., p. 598.
p. 92 "I think there is no doubt . . ." Merrill, op. cit., p. 316.
p. 92 ". . . We cannot allow the Indians . . ." Merrill, op. cit., p. 351.
p. 92 ". . . until at least ten Indians . . ." Marszalek, op. cit., p. 389.
p. 92 ". . . he acted like a boy turned loose . . ." Lewis, op. cit., p. 596.
p. 94 "I like American scenery . . ." Lewis, op. cit., p. 612.
p. 94 "I think we understand . . ." Lewis, op. cit., p. 635.
p. 97 ". . . the people high and low . . ." Merrill, op. cit., p. 377.
p. 97 "Please decline any nomination . . ." Lewis, op. cit., p. 631.
p. 97 "Your name is the only one . . ." Lewis, op. cit., p. 631.
p. 98 "Wait for me, Ellen . . ." Lewis, op. cit., p. 645.
p. 98 "If I were in his place . . ." Marszalek, op. cit., p. 496.
p. 100 "When all is said . . ." Marszalek, op. cit., p. 495.

BIBLIOGRAPHY

Athearn, Robert. *William Tecumseh Sherman and the Settlement of the West*. Oklahoma: University of Oklahoma Press, 1956.

Coburn, Mark. *Terrible Innocence: General Sherman at War*. New York: Hippocrene Books, 1993.

Foote, Shelby. *Civil War*. New York: Random House, 1974.

Hart, B. H. Liddell. *Sherman: Soldier, Realist, American*. New York: Frederick Praeger, 1958.

Lewis, Lloyd. *Sherman: Fighting Prophet*. New York: Harcourt, Brace and Company, 1932.

Kerr, Laura. *William Tecumseh Sherman: A Family Chronicle*. Lancaster. Fairfield Heritage Association, 1984.

Marszalek, John. *Sherman: A Soldier's Passion for Order*. New York: The Free Press, 1993.

Merrill, James. *William Tecumseh Sherman*. Chicago: Rand McNally & Co., 1971.

Sherman, William T. *Memoirs of General William T. Sherman*. Bloomington: Indiana University Press, 1957.

Stein, R. Conrad. *The Story of Gold at Sutter's Mill*. Chicago: Children's Press, 1981.

INDEX

Abolitionists, 15, 17, 30, 57
Alden, Admiral, 94
Alleghany Mountains, 63
Appomattox Courthouse, 83
Arkansas Post, Battle of, 50
Arkansas River, 48
Atlanta Constitution, 100
Atlanta, Georgia, 64-65, 67, 70, 80
Arthur, President Chester A., 94

Beauregard, General Pierre, 38
Brown, John, 31
Buell, Major D. C., 30
Bull Run, Battle of, 38-40, 62
Burnside, General Ambrose, 59

California Gold Rush, 20
Cameron, Simon, 41-42, 47
Canby, General Edward, 88
Charleston, South Carolina, 17, 36, 80
Chattahoochie River, 66

Cheyennes, 92
Chickasaw, Battle of, 49-50
Conduct of the War Committee, 88
Columbia, South Carolina, 80-81

Dartmouth College, 96
Davis, Jefferson, 34, 84, 87
Democratic Party, 68
Dred Scott, 31
Durham Station, North Carolina, 84

Emancipation Proclamation, 52
Ewing, Maria, 11-12
Ewing, Thomas, 11-12, 14, 28, 30, 76

Fifteenth Amendment, 96
Fort Donelson, 44
Fort McAlister, 76
Fort Sumter, 36, 49, 82

Goldsboro, North Carolina, 83
Grant, General Ulysses S. 44, 49, 54, 63, 68, 70, 78, 83, 88-90, 93

Halleck, General Henry, 43-44, 47, 87
Hardee, General William, 74, 76
Hayes, President Rutherford B., 96
Hood, General John Bell, 66-67

Indian Commission, 91

Jackson, President Andrew, 12
Johnson, President Andrew, 88-89, 91
Johnson, Governor J. Neely, 26
Johnston, General Joseph P., 54-57, 66, 80, 82-84, 86-87, 98

Kirby-Smith, General, 88

Lee, General Robert E., 70, 83
Lincoln, President Abraham, 31, 33-34, 36, 39, 41, 52, 60, 68, 70, 74, 76, 83-84, 86, 89
Louisiana Military Seminary, 30-32, 34

McClellan, General George B., 42, 68
Mexican-American War, 18-19
Milldgeville, Georgia, 74
Mississippi River, 40, 52, 63
Moore, Governor Thomas, 33-34

Navahoes, 92

Ogallalas, 92
Ogeechee River, 74

Park, Mayor John, 48
Pemberton, General John, 53-54
Princeton University, 96
Promontory Point, Utah, 93

Richmond, Virginia, 70, 87

Savannah, Georgia, 68, 74, 76, 78-79, 87
Scott, General Winfield, 20
Seminoles, 16, 92
Sherman, Charles, 9
Sherman, Charles Ewing, 76-77, 98
Sherman, Ellen Ewing, 15, 18-19, 22-24, 30, 32-33, 36, 43, 47, 50, 54, 56-57, 65, 67, 88-89, 92, 97-98
Sherman, James, 11
Sherman, John, 11, 18, 26, 32, 34,

43, 76
Sherman, Mary, 11, 14
Sherman, Mary Elizabeth, 23
Sherman, Maria (Minnie) Ewing, 22-24
Sherman, Philemon Tecumseh, 92
Sherman, Taylor, 11
Sherman, Thomas Ewing, 28, 60, 88-89
Sherman, William (Willie) Ewing, 26, 56, 98
Sherman, William Tecumseh
  birth, 9
  childhood, 10-13
  father's death, 11
  as surveyor, 12, 20
  at West Point, 13-15
  enters army, 16
  attitude toward slavery, 17-18, 26, 31
  as quartermaster, 19, 22
  and military life, 19-20, 22-23
  marriage, 22
  promoted to captain, 22
  resigns from army, 24
  as banker, 24-28
  in California State miliitia, 26, 28
  as lawyer, 30
  as school superintendent, 30-34
  opinion of Civil War
  rejoins army, 36
  at Bull Run, 38-39
  attitude toward press, 39, 42
  attitude toward foraging, 40
  called insane, 40-44
  at Shiloh, 44, 46, 47
  at Memphis, 48-49
  Vicksburg campaign, 49-50, 52-54
  as destroyer, 54, 56, 62-63
  promoted to Bridger General, 56
  attitude toward black soliders, 57
  Tennesse campaign, 58-60
  march on Atlanta, 64-67
  attitude toward politics, 68
  march on Savannah, 70, 72, 74, 76
  "Smoky March," 80-83
  accepts Johnston's surrender, 84, 86
  conflict with Edwin Stanton, 86-89
  on Indian Commission, 91-92
  as railroad supervisor, 93
  as Chief of Army, 93-94, 96-97
  tours Europe, 94
  as public speaker, 89-90, 94
  as writer, 94, 96

declines Republican nomination
    for President, 96-97
  receives honory degrees, 96
  tours South, 97
  retires from army, 97
  death, 98
  funeral, 98, 100
Shiloh, Battle of, 46-47, 49
Sioux, 92
Slavery, 11, 15-18, 26, 30-32
Stanton, Edwin, 86-89, 91

Tennesse River, 58
Thirteenth Regular Infantry, 36
Tilden, Samuel, 96

Underground Railroad, 30-31
USS Lexington, 19

Vicksburg, Mississippi, 49, 52-54,
    62

West Point, 12-15, 17, 30, 37, 96
Whippy Swamp, 80,
Wool, Gen-eral, 28

Yale University, 96

PHOTO CREDITS

21, 25, 27, 55, 71 (bottom), The Archives of the University of Notre Dame; 29, 53, 75, 78, 85, National Archives; 35, 45, 51, 56, 61, 69, 71 (top), 73, 77, 95, 99, The Library of Congress.